Crossing the Line

Extending Young People's Access to Cultural Venues

with funding by

CALOUSTE
GULBENKIAN
FOUNDATION

THE **ARTS COUNCIL**
OF ENGLAND

Crossing the Line

Extending Young People's Access to Cultural Venues

Edited by John Harland and Kay Kinder

CALOUSTE GULBENKIAN FOUNDATION, LONDON

Published by the
Calouste Gulbenkian Foundation
United Kingdom Branch
98 Portland Place
London W1N 4ET
Tel: 020 7636 5313

ISBN 0 903319 91 8

British Library Cataloguing-in-Publication Data
A catalogue record for this book is available from the
British Library

Designed by Andrew Shoolbred
Printed by Expression Printers Ltd, IP23 8HH

Distributed by Turnaround Publisher Services Ltd, Unit 3,
Olympia Trading Estate, Coburg Road, Wood Green, London
N22 6TZ. Tel: 020 8829 3000, Fax: 020 8881 5088, E-mail:
orders@turnaround-uk.com

**Copies of this document are available in alternative
formats from the Education and Employment
Department at the Arts Council of England, 14 Great
Peter Street, London SW1P 3NQ. Tel: 020 7973 6551,
Fax: 020 7973 6833, Minicom: 020 7973 6564**

Cover photograph: Artswork 'Off the Wall'. Photo: John Heywood.
Anthony Caro, *Woman Waking Up*

Contents

Abbreviations

A4E	Arts For Everyone
ACE	Arts Council of England
ACGB	Arts Council of Great Britain
AMCo	Northern Arts Marketing
CGF	Calouste Gulbenkian Foundation
DCMS	Department for Culture, Media and Sport
DES	Department of Education and Science
DfEE	Department for Education and Employment
DNH	Department of National Heritage
GLA	Greater London Arts
HMSO	Her Majesty's Stationery Office
HRC	Harris Research Centre
INSET	In-service Education and Training of Teachers
MAX	Marketing the Arts in Oxfordshire
NACCCE	National Advisory Committee on Creative and Cultural Education
NCA	National Campaign for the Arts
NCC	National Curriculum Council
NFER	National Foundation for Educational Research
NYA	National Youth Agency
RAB	Regional Arts Board
RSA	Royal Society for the Encouragement of Arts, Manufactures and Commerce
RSGB	Research Services of Great Britain
RTS	Rural Touring Scheme
SAC	Scottish Arts Council
SEU	Social Exclusion Unit

The Authors

Mary Ashworth is a Research Officer with NFER. Formerly a teacher of English and drama, her recent research has included a baseline evaluation of CAPE UK (Creative Arts Partnerships in Education) and a longitudinal study of pupil perspectives on the curriculum.

Karen Halsey is an Assistant Research Officer at the NFER Northern Office. Previously, she was employed at a drugs counselling service for young people. Her recent research has included projects on truancy, exclusions and the arts.

John Harland is Head of NFER's Northern Office in York. Formerly a teacher, he has contributed to several studies in the arts area, including *Arts in Their View*. He is currently conducting research into the effects and effectiveness of arts education in schools.

Kay Kinder is a Principal Researcher Officer at the NFER Northern Office. Initially a primary teacher, she carried out research into primary education. With NFER, she has published in the fields of professional development, the arts and, especially, pupil disaffection.

Stephanie Pitts is a Lecturer in Music at the University of Sheffield, where she runs a distance-learning MA course in Psychology for Musicians. She is the author of *A Century of Change in Music Education*.

Sara Selwood is a Principal Lecturer and Researcher at the University of Westminster. Much of her work focuses on museums and galleries, in particular visitor studies and education programmes. She is the co-author of various studies on the subsidised cultural sector and also edits *Cultural Trends*.

Authors' Acknowledgements

The authors would like to offer their thanks to those who gave particular support to the production of this report. We are especially grateful to the 20 young people who gave their time to be interviewed; and to all those within cultural organisations and venues who offered examples of their work with young people. We would also like to thank Pauline Benefield and her colleagues at NFER library in Slough for their invaluable support work on the literature review, and the secretarial staff in NFER's Northern Office for helping ensure deadlines were met.

All the readers of the report's initial draft (who are cited in the foreword) also deserve our grateful acknowledgement.

Finally, each author would wish to express their special appreciation of the contribution of Norinne Betjemann and Simon Richey, who have provided invaluable support, advice and insights throughout the project's lifespan – from its conception to final publication.

Foreword

Young people between the ages of fourteen and eighteen, research suggests, are often disinclined to visit such cultural venues as theatres, concert halls, galleries and museums. It is possible for a young person to experience only a fleeting acquaintance with venues of this kind and to cease to visit them subsequently, not necessarily because they dislike a particular art form but because these cultural venues do not appear to offer what is relevant to them. As a result of this assumption and lack of involvement, young people may be denied the possibility of informed choice. How can venues, schools and others help young people to consider a wider spectrum of cultural experiences?

The purpose of this report, commissioned jointly by the Gulbenkian Foundation and the Arts Council of England, is to open up this issue and encourage debate. While we acknowledge that much good work is being done to bring young people and venues closer together – to make it easier for them to cross that invisible line of our title – there is much that still remains to be done. We see this report as a preliminary to further discussion, further research and further action.

John Harland, Kay Kinder, Mary Ashworth, Karen Halsey, Stephanie Pitts and Sara Selwood have researched, analysed and presented the issues and we are grateful for their hard work and commitment. In addition, we would like to thank the following people who read the report in draft stage and offered many useful comments and suggestions: Jillian Barker, Julia Calver, Vic Ecclestone, Giles Elliott, Jenny Harris, Naomi Horlock, Christine Jackson, Dianne Jefferson, Hugh James, Tony Knight, David Leighton, Abigail Moss, Nick Randell, Shabnam Shabazi, Fahmida Shah, Ann Stephens, Pauline Tambling, Christopher Thomson, and Zelda Wilkins.

Simon Richey
Assistant Director (Education)
Calouste Gulbenkian Foundation
(UK Branch)

Norinne Betjemann
Education and Employment Officer
Education and Employment Department
Arts Council of England

Executive Summary

1. INTRODUCTION

(pages 15–18)

The report begins by proposing that in order to develop effective strategies for extending young people's access to cultural venues, it may first be necessary to conduct a detailed and wide-ranging analysis of the complex problems involved. As a precursor to such an analysis, this report reviews the available research evidence (Chapter 2), describes some current initiatives (Chapter 3), and explores accounts from a small sample of young people (Chapter 4). Examining the problems and opportunities involved in broadening young people's access to both high and popular culture – a two-way culture – the report concentrates on the 14–18 age range and cultural venues that are known to be associated with limited attendance by young people. Its focus is specifically on the 'audience' role, though the critical and participatory nature of this role is recognised as an integral part of the whole gamut of types of engagement in the arts and culture.

2. A REVIEW OF THE LITERATURE

(pages 19–38)

The review found that recent research and policy papers have highlighted the participatory end of the spectrum, with young people's 'audience' roles considered much more rarely. While there are many valid reasons for this emphasis, the goal of cultural inclusion would also seem to demand the development and application of the listening, viewing and critical skills necessary for audience access as well.

The research evidence demonstrated that attendance at cultural venues declines as children progress through their teens. The mid-teens appear to be associated with particularly low levels of audience involvement. Generally, males and young people from semi-skilled or unskilled backgrounds were more likely to be non-attenders than girls or middle-class teenagers. Parental influence was found to be an important factor in encouraging involvement. There was a lack of unequivocal evidence on the extent to which schools imparted a positive effect on young people's attendance at cultural venues and on the nature of the curriculum and teaching approaches most likely to achieve these results.

The existing literature indicated that increasing young people's access to cultural organisations necessitates the overcoming of physical barriers, such as cost, travel and lack of time, and, most importantly, psychological barriers, especially perceptions that the arts are irrelevant and culturally exclusive.

3. AN ILLUSTRATIVE AUDIT OF RECENT INITIATIVES
(pages 39–63)

The audit seeks to identify the marketing strategies deployed by initiatives which aim to attract 14–18 year olds to cultural institutions across all art forms. Data for the audit were collected through telephone discussions with staff at the respective venues, supplemented by relevant documentation. The audit in no way intends to be evaluative, rather to illuminate significant discernible trends.

Marketing strategies could be seen to range along a continuum, high-lighting to varying degrees the 'extrinsic' or 'intrinsic' appeal of an event or venue. The 'extrinsic' category referred to material incentives, such as ticket schemes, and the marketing medium, where 'street credibility' was all important. The 'intrinsic' category referred to the relevance of the art form itself to young people's own culture, and the relevance of the content to their interests and concerns.

Most initiatives attempted to attract young people by stimulating their interest through some form of participation, beforehand or during the event itself. According to respondents, other successful strategies for engaging the commitment of a younger audience included scrupulous consultation, recognition of the need for relevance, and the capacity to sustain momentum secured by long-term funding.

4. 'I AM NEW': YOUNG PEOPLE'S ACCOUNTS OF ACCESSING CULTURAL VENUES
(pages 64–101)

How a sample of 20 young people, aged 14–18, viewed and experienced cultural venues is recounted in this chapter, with particular attention given to the language they used. Not surprisingly, most expressed the view that venues such as art galleries, heritage, museums, dance and music concerts were 'not for young people', citing typical audiences as old/middle-aged, affluent or specialist enthusiasts. Most could attest to enjoying any visit they did make; though, significantly, a number mentioned a sense of apprehension prior to an encounter. Equally, low-level attenders were those who had fewer comments and vaguer descriptions to offer about cultural venues.

Helping young people develop this audience language and positive antici-pation may thus be an issue. In contrast, high attenders often expressed the intense physical power and presence of their audience experience and the fun of audience membership. Outcomes such as new knowledge, psycho-logical well being and motivation to revisit venues were also mentioned in some instances. The sample's perceived barriers to attendance reaffirmed much previous research (e.g. difficulties of access, non-appropriate content, peer pressure, stereotypical views from the media). Their recommendations for improving young people's access included better advertising and promo-tion; more opportunities for young people to socialise at the venues; an adapted content (such as shorter performances, more activity/interaction, themes that appeal to young people); works performed or created by young people; and relocation to venues familiar to them. Opportunity was the key: as one young person put it, 'You have got to go once to understand what it's about.'

5. CULTURAL MENTORS?

(pages 102–105)

This section looks at the concept of 'cultural mentor/mediator' as a poten-tially important strategy for increasing young people's access to cultural venues. Evidence from the literature review, the research and the audit suggests the value of such a role. Using examples and models from both English and American mentoring schemes, the report concludes that cultural mentoring requires further exploration, piloting and evaluation. Nevertheless, given all the evidence on young people's attendance, this strategy appears to offer a greater likelihood of success than relying on mere curricular entitlements as a means of widening access to cultural venues.

6. AREAS OF FURTHER ENQUIRY: CONCLUDING STATEMENT

(pages 106–108)

The report ends with a concluding statement from the Gulbenkian Foundation and the Arts Council of England where a series of broad state-ments and questions are posed designed to stimulate further debate.

INTRODUCTION

John Harland and Kay Kinder

In a paper exploring the role of young people in the interface between 'popular culture' and the 'institutional culture' of the high arts, Simon Richey concluded:

> ... I believe that young people are entitled to the benefits, the pleasures, the insights of all of culture and not just a part of it. I would wish that those who have experience only of popular culture are given the opportunity to taste something different and to have their cultural horizons enlarged; just as I would hope that the young person who knows only high culture, is given the opportunity to taste something different also. And it is because I believe that these journeys between cultures are made easier if the cultures themselves adapt and adjust that I have emphasised the importance of borrowing of practice, this two-way process, this two-way culture. (1996:12)

Research evidence, however, would suggest that this vision is well in advance of the reality on the ground. The NFER study *Arts in Their View* (Harland et al., 1995), for example, indicated very limited involvement on the part of young people in the institutional culture of the high arts, particularly among certain social groups. Anecdotally, the researchers found that it was not uncommon to interview young people who had never been inside a theatre or an art gallery. What, then, can be done to make good this apparent shortfall between the kind of aspirations espoused by Richey and the current reality of young people's patterns of cultural behaviour?

In general terms, at least, official bodies have not been dormant in this area. During the last five years, the Department for Culture, Media and Sport (DCMS) and its predecessor, the Department of National Heritage (DNH), have sought to encourage young people's involvement in cultural organisations such as theatres, galleries, music groups and museums, not least as part of its access initiatives (GB. DNH, 1996). More recently, the DCMS has published reports on widening access to museums (GB. DCMS, 1999a) and on the role of the arts and sports in combating social exclusion (GB. DCMS, 1999b). It has also been influential in the establishment of the National Foundation for Youth Music. Additionally, the Department for Education and Employment (DfEE) has launched the music standards fund and has started promoting educational partnerships between schools, arts organisations and museums (e.g. study support projects, GB. DfEE, 1998).

Various bodies supported by the DCMS have also been active in promoting young people's involvement with cultural venues. These include the Arts Council of England (ACE) – most notably in its capacity as a lottery distributor (see Rider, 1997; Harris Qualitative, 1997) and its New Audiences programme, which, with £5 million annual funding from DCMS, aims to create new audiences for the arts among young people in particular (ACE, 1998 and 1999).

Notwithstanding the laudable intentions behind these initiatives, questions can be raised as to whether they are commensurate with the scale and complexities of the problems involved. For instance, has sufficient thought been devoted to the specific challenges of widening young people's access to cultural venues in an audience role, as distinct, say, from the general goal of encouraging youth participation in the arts? Without pre-judging the evaluation of such initiatives as the New Audiences programme (the report on which was not available at the time of this review), is it likely that single arts events by themselves can achieve sustainable changes in young people's cultural behaviour? With a view to laying down the foundations for the cultural inclusion of future generations of young people, has enough consideration been given to the essential features of a coherent curriculum that would prepare young people for their adult lives in cultural terms? Accordingly, it is tentatively suggested that in order to succeed in increasing young people's access to cultural venues, policies and initiatives may need to be based on a more fundamental and wide-ranging analysis than has hitherto been undertaken.

This report does not attempt to offer such an analysis. Instead, by exploring the available research evidence (Chapter 2), current initiatives (Chapter 3), and accounts from a small sample of young people (Chapter 4), it endeavours to raise some of the issues and opportunities that a wider examination may subsequently consider in more detail.

Wherever possible, young people in the 14 to 18 age range have been the particular focus of attention. There are a number of reasons for concentrating on this age span. Previous research has suggested that this group is especially under-represented at cultural venues. The mid-teens are often seen as a critical period in the process of identity formation. There is also the advantage that this range incorporates young people within and beyond the years of compulsory schooling. In practice, it proved impossible to restrict the review of the research literature and the audit of types of initiative to this particular age band. Consequently, the first two chapters include much material that pertains to 'young people' broadly defined or within the age categories of 11 to 24. The interview programme was reserved for teenagers in the 14 to 18 span.

For current purposes, the emphasis has been placed on 'cultural venues' that are known to be associated with limited attendance by young people. In the main, these have comprised theatres, art galleries, museums, concert venues, arts centres, festivals, poetry-readings and performances of dance and opera. In view of their specialist nature, libraries were not included. Perhaps more controversially, cinemas also tended to be excluded on the grounds that attendance levels are comparatively high among this age range – though unfortunately, this has resulted in the removal of 'art films' and 'art cinemas' from the analysis. Similar problems were encountered over various genres of popular music concerts.

Essentially, the report is concerned with young people in an audience role, using terms such as 'non-participant' and 'consumer-oriented' to cover all engagement in the arts that is receptive and critical, rather than producer-oriented and participatory – though clearly, all these concepts are closely interrelated and perhaps should be seen as different points on a continuum of different types of engagement in the arts. It is acknowledged that, in considering young people's attendance at cultural venues, we are dealing with a limited sub-set of audience roles. As Willis (1990) has observed, the whole notion of 'audience' has undergone radical changes in recent decades, so that live human performances may have 'disappeared from the centre' in favour of 'single artefacts which are then commodified as pop songs, videos, films and distributed to widely distributed "audiences" through the cultural media'. Thus, while focusing here on involvement in collective audiences, it is recognised that many other types of audience role will need to be included in a comprehensive agenda for the cultural education of young people. Similarly, there is no suggestion here that the act of being a spectator or member of an audience is inherently a passive role. Willis (1990) has demonstrated that cultural 'consumption' can be transformed by young people into creative 'producer' activities (e.g. by dubbing and mixing commercially recorded music) and Downing (1999) has examined how theatre audiences, for example, assume participatory roles in shaping the nature and quality of the live performance experienced. From such perspectives, it can be seen that efforts to help prepare young people for audience roles may also address the associated aim of developing the quality of audiences themselves, which in turn, if Downing's analysis is correct, encourages the production of enhanced cultural outcomes in the future. Thus, for all these reasons – personal, social and cultural development – issues surrounding the rate of young people's attendance at cultural venues and the quality of their performance as members of an audience assume considerable importance.

As a final word of introduction, it is worth acknowledging that objections may exist to the fundamental aim of this report, with its implied premise that increasing access to cultural organisations is a potentially beneficial outcome. Willis (1990) and Hill (1997) are among recent writers who have championed the cause of 'youth arts' as a genre distinct from the arts experiences currently available in established cultural organisations, with

Hill suggesting that there is 'frustrated social manipulation' in inviting young people to 'join our world' by participating in mainstream arts. Viewing young people as 'an indicator of our social health', Hill suggests that the search for identity that, for him, epitomises the adolescent years, should not be forced into the mould of adult arts experiences, but should be valued in its own terms as the 'artistry of growth'.

Willis appears to give similarly low status to the aim of increasing access to cultural organisations, stating that a 'democratisation of the arts' is the only route towards making the arts relevant to young people. In practice, this means the recognition of commercial and mass culture as being aesthetically significant, with graffiti, fashion, image and style allowing young people to form a 'personalised cultural map'. Nonetheless, set against these objections are the testimonies of teachers, artists and young people (Whitfield, 1991; Harland et al., 1995; RSA, 1997) about the value of participation in the 'high' arts and, more rarely, of attendance at arts events. Clearly, arts organisations can learn from the strategies of community artists, and from the cultural preferences and 'meaning-making' of young people, but to perpetuate a rigid dividing line between 'youth/popular' and 'adult/high' arts is unlikely to benefit either party. Indeed, to be fair, Willis does see scope in fostering the interface between cultural venues and the young, so long as the latter are not treated as merely the marketing targets of audience development campaigns, but are given opportunities to share in the re-defining and regeneration of high arts institutions.

Accordingly, the premise adopted here is that, while fully respecting that there are young people who not feel the need to engage with the arts at all, Richey's notion of a 'two-way culture' represents a vital and valid aim of creative and cultural education. A similar position is adopted in the recent National Advisory Committee on Creative and Cultural Education report, when it challenges the assumption that:

> ...there is an unbridgeable gap between high art and popular culture. We think this assumption is wrong for two reasons. The first is that there is in practice an interaction and overlap between different cultural processes, including high art and popular culture. The second is that many people enjoy and contribute to both, as informed and dynamic audiences and makers.
> (GB.DfEE.DCMS.NACCCE, 1999:41)

A REVIEW OF THE LITERATURE

2

Stephanie Pitts, John Harland and Sara Selwood

2.1 INTRODUCTION: EDUCATION FOR THE AUDIENCE ROLE

This review considers three aspects of young people's relationships with cultural venues:

- their attendance at cultural venues;
- their attitudes and barriers to attendance;
- the role of schools, families and cultural organisations in encouraging young people's attendance.

References are made to various policy documents and research reports, most of which have appeared since 1990. With the exception of some sources that draw on North American literature, the majority of references are to British publications.

Probably the most conspicuous feature of the literature is that recent research on young people's involvement in the arts has concentrated on participatory activities, with 'spectator', 'consumer' or 'audience' roles considered more rarely. Likewise, while the benefits to young people of participation in the arts have frequently been discussed, few attempts have been made to analyse the reasons why young people do or do not visit cultural organisations. Adopting Gardner's (1973) terminology, research into young people and the arts (e.g. Ings, 1998) has tended to concentrate on the 'making system' rather than either the 'perceiving system' or the 'feeling system'. Or to use Wilson's (1997) concepts, research into youth arts has focused more on involvement in 'art production' rather than on 'aesthetics', 'art criticism' or 'art history'.

Similarly, policy reports published since the Education Reform Act of 1988 have argued the case for arts (Campaign for Music in the Curriculum, 1998; Rogers, 1995a) predominantly on the grounds of the gains to be achieved through active participation in the arts. In line with this tendency, the NACCCE report (GB. DfEE. DCMS. NACCCE, 1999) also accentuates participatory involvement and makes only passing references to the development of young people's audience roles. The report recognises the importance of evaluative judgement-making to the creative process and advocates the dissemination of some examples of initiatives to extend young people's access to cultural venues (e.g. performance passes, arts miles schemes, trusts which give money to pupils to attend cultural events). Interestingly, however, such initiatives are only cited under 'funding strategies' (ibid:146). Education for the audience role is not addressed in the sections on curriculum, pedagogy and assessment. Few would seriously question the strong emphasis given to the participatory dimension within the report, especially given its wide-ranging creative and cultural remit, its sociological rather than artistic definition of 'culture' and the priority it places on preparing young people for their future economic rather than leisure roles. Nevertheless, what is noticeable is the limited extent to which the report considers the contribution that schools and cultural organisations can give to developing discriminating audiences at cultural venues, as a vehicle for sustaining creative and cultural education beyond the age of compulsory schooling. This possible oversight seems particularly surprising in view of the report's avouched commitment to lifelong learning.

The apparent dominance of the participatory role in any discussion of the arts is a reflection of trends in education that have moved away from 'appreciation'-based teaching towards more active and creative arts learning in the latter quarter of this century. While the National Curriculum includes references to appraising music, appreciating dance, critical studies in art and responding to drama, practical involvement and participatory outcomes in the arts seem to remain the priority for most teachers (Harland et al., 1998). Many of the texts considered in this review fail to mention the role of the audience or critic at all, except in the context of providing 'ideas and resource material' for future participation (ACGB, 1993). Furthermore, it tends to be the public performances of the arts that are celebrated in schools (Secondary Heads Association, 1998). For teachers and pupils, there are many valid reasons for this focus, but the goal of cultural inclusion would also seem to demand the development of listening, viewing and critical skills necessary for audience access, as well as an awareness that audiences too make a vital contribution to arts experiences and cultural creativity.

2.2 YOUNG PEOPLE'S ATTENDANCE AT CULTURAL VENUES

The data on young people's attendances at cultural venues are far from comprehensive. The most detailed generic surveys of youth participation in the arts in recent years have been O'Brien's (1996) MORI research and the NFER (Harland et al., 1995) *Arts in Their View* report. Both of these had a broad remit, taking a wide definition of the arts, and focusing on all engagement, not specifically the audience role.

O'Brien collected questionnaire responses from 4,532 pupils aged 11 to 16. The survey included questions on arts attendance 'as part of a school trip' and 'outside school (e.g. with family or friends)'. These revealed a high level of cinema attendance outside school (72 per cent), with much lower attendance at plays (31 per cent), musical (not rock or pop) events (11 per cent), ballet (9 per cent), poetry readings (5 per cent) and opera (4 per cent). Figures for arts attendance were all higher outside school than during school hours.

The type of cultural venue visited as part of school trips revealed an emphasis on 'information gathering' expeditions, rather than purely arts-focused occasions. A school outing to a museum, for example, was more likely to be connected with the history syllabus than with an arts subject, although O'Brien's data could give no further insight on the motivation for attendance. She does report, however, that of those young people who had attended arts events, with school or in their own time, the majority had enjoyed the experience, although the figure for arts festivals was notably lower (around 50 per cent). While the influence of school is acknowledged as significant, the dominant educational culture remains one of participation, with audience roles having a lower profile:

> *Overall a high percentage of school children attend what can be termed 'arts and cultural events and activities' although in specific artform areas the percentage attending tends to be lower than the percentage participating. Hence school children are more likely to do than attend.*
> (O'Brien, 1996:28)

Harland et al. present findings that are often consistent with O'Brien's, drawn from semi-structured interviews with a random sample of around 700 14–24 year olds. Again, the report focuses mainly on participation, offering only a short chapter on arts attendance. Unlike the O'Brien survey, which invited respondents to tick appropriate activities from a predetermined list (a technique which generally elicits higher responses), the relevant evidence in the NFER study was derived from an open-ended item that asked interviewees to identify any arts experiences they had encountered over the past year. As might be expected, daytime encounters with the arts among the school-aged population were dominated by literature (42 per cent), with theatre visits (8 per cent), art galleries (7 per cent) and listening to recorded music (7 per cent) leading the remaining smaller categories.

In leisure time across the full spectrum of ages in the study, cinema was the most frequently visited venue (29 per cent), but listening to various styles of music was mentioned more often (40 per cent), followed by reading literature (30 per cent). Other leisure-time attendance rates (for the full age range) signalled a very limited degree of involvement in the type of cultural events being considered here: the theatre (19 per cent), galleries (7 per cent), live classical (2 per cent), and dance/ballet (2 per cent).

Both of these studies identified some variations by gender. In the O'Brien survey, girls were more active than boys in out-of-school attendance at most venues. Likewise, Harland et al. found that, compared to their male peers, females in the 14–24 age range were more likely to be theatre-goers.

Most significantly for our purposes, the two studies exposed some pertinent variations by age. The results from the O'Brien survey were consistent with the view that as teenagers progress from 11 to 16 they become more likely to go to the cinema and rock concerts out of school, but less likely to attend theatres, galleries, museums, and dance performances. Hence, the 14–16 phase was associated with lower attendance at 'high' cultural venues than earlier ages. The NFER study also found that the 14–16 group had the lowest proportions attending such venues out of school. For three art forms (theatre, galleries and literature) there were signs of increased engagement as young people progressed from 17 to 24, but in the 17–20 age range limited involvement in audience roles was still very evident: fewer than one in five reported attending a theatre, one in 12 had been to a gallery, one in 33 had attended live classical music and one in 100 mentioned going to a dance performance.

Unfortunately, neither of these sources shows the rates of in-school attendance at cultural venues broken down by ages, so it is not possible to ascertain whether involvement in school trips increases or declines over the secondary school phase. The review could find no evidence that school-inspired attendance was higher during key stage 3 than key stage 4, nor that such visits were more likely to be arranged for those studying arts-based GCSE courses at key stage 4 than those who were not. Without these data, the schools' role in encouraging cultural inclusion is very difficult to evaluate. Indeed, as we shall see later, the existing research evidence is so scant that it is not possible to determine with confidence whether school-supported visits have a positive or deleterious effect on young people's attitudes and behaviour towards attending cultural venues.

It was clear from the NFER study that attendance at such venues was heavily influenced by social class. By way of illustration, relative to young people from skilled or semi-skilled backgrounds, young people with parents in professional occupations were twice as likely to be theatre-goers, three times more likely to go to live classical performances and seven times more likely to attend dance performances.

For the most part, the absence of comparable evidence from large-scale general surveys makes it impossible to corroborate the findings from these two studies against broader data-sets. However, survey evidence presented in *Social Trends* (GB. Office for National Statistics, 1999) indicated that 14 per cent of 16–24 year olds said they had attended a theatre in their leisure time in the three months prior to interviews conducted in 1997–98. This corresponds quite closely to the 19 per cent of 14–24 year olds who had attended a theatre in their leisure time during the previous 12 months in Harland et al., especially if allowance is made for the different timescales offered to interviewees.

The information supplied by the O'Brien and *Arts in Their View* studies can be supplemented by some more focused research into attendance patterns for specific art forms or in particular regions of the country. For example, according to museum visitor surveys, those aged 16–24 are among the smallest group attending. While visitor profiles vary considerably from museum to museum, an analysis of 106 visitor surveys suggests that this group represents less than 14 per cent of museum visitors (Davies 1994).

Recent System Three research (1998), commissioned by the Scottish Arts Council, replicated the finding that going to the cinema is the most popular arts activity (68 per cent), followed by 'musicals/pantomimes/variety shows' (55 per cent) and 'galleries/museums' (53 per cent). However, the results were not broken down by age, and so insight into the behaviour of young people in Scotland is limited.

The Mass Observation (1990) survey of 'users and non-users' of the arts in Greater London offers another point of comparison, with its combination of nine group interviews and 1,042 individual interviews yielding substantial data on levels of attendance and reasons for doing so. The cinema was once again rated as the most frequently attended venue (49 per cent). Of the cultural venues attended, museums (34 per cent) and theatre (34 per cent) occupied the next highest rankings, with less than one in five (17 per cent) going to classical concerts, and only one in ten going to opera (11 per cent), ballet (10 per cent) or jazz (10 per cent).

The *Youth Audience Research Report* (ACE, 1994) focuses primarily on the theatre. Data were collected through 389 questionnaires in 1994, with follow-up interviews with 18 respondents, which were linked more closely with the collaborating venues, Nottingham Playhouse and the Nuffield Theatre, Southampton. The involvement of these two institutions complicates the data somewhat, with the sample divided into mutually exclusive groups who, within the last twelve months, had attended either of the specific theatres, had attended live stage performances elsewhere, or had been to arts events other than the theatre. Like O'Brien, the ACE-commissioned researchers found the cinema to be the most popular venue among all three groups, with the first two 'stagegoing' groups more likely to have attended a variety of arts events.

Performances, with the exception of dance, are shown by the ACE research to be more attractive to the 16–24 age group than galleries and exhibitions, although the clear bias of the questionnaire towards 'events' rather than 'places' may have influenced this result. When respondents were asked to sort a series of value statements about the theatre, a generally positive image emerged, although views on value for money were strongly polarised. This would again seem to support O'Brien's view that those young people who attend arts events enjoy them, although the ACE research is more ambivalent in its support of school theatre outings, stating that 'at worst these trips had acted as aversion therapy in which school-children had been subjected to a play they did not understand and had used the experience as a rationalisation for avoiding theatre ever since'.

The complexity of the emerging picture demonstrates that a closer look at the attitudes, influences and barriers that impact upon young people's arts attendance is essential, and the fragmentary information available within the literature will be considered next.

2.3 ATTITUDES AND BARRIERS TO ATTENDANCE

Of the quantitative reports discussed so far, many include qualitative elements, which investigate the motives, attitudes and barriers that affect young people's engagement with the arts. A variety of research methodologies have been used, and justifications for each of them appear in the literature, along with evidence of their potential weaknesses. The methods of psychodrawing and picture completion advocated by Cooper and Tower (1992) are rarely found, with researchers more often using questionnaires (e.g. AMCo, 1993), group discussions (e.g. Mass Observation, 1990), interviews (e.g. System Three, 1998) or a mixture of techniques (e.g. Moore, 1997). The relative merits of different methodologies could be argued at length, but it is sufficient to say that the difficulties in accumulating evidence of attitudes to audience engagement in the arts are considerable.

In their overview of young people's attitudes to the arts, broadcasting, sport and heritage, and in earlier NFER research, Harland et al. (1995 and 1996) identify a number of categories into which positive and negative attitudes to the arts can be placed, while acknowledging that a 'cluster of motives' are most likely to influence any decisions about cultural venues. Harland et al.'s (1996) proposed categories of motivation include 'task-orientated/knowledge-seeking', 'socialising', 'physiological/therapeutic', and 'intrinsic/aesthetic', while barriers are identified as including perceived 'talent'(or lack of it), 'lack of relevance/comfortability' and 'image'.

The *Arts in Their View* study (Harland et al., 1995) identified the attitudes of young people according to factors of low, medium and high level motivation, stating that perceptions of the arts as having 'status-seeking', 'monetary' or 'achievement-oriented' motives were the least likely to sustain active involvement. Attitudes more typically associated with audience (but probably not active participant) engagement with the arts fell into the low or medium motivation categories, including 'general/enjoyment'; 'social pressure'; 'relevance/comfortability'; and 'situation-specific'. Audiences tend to expect a sociable, enjoyable experience when they attend an arts venue, and indeed the Mass Observation survey reports 82 per cent agree-ment that the arts should 'leave you feeling happy' (Mass Observation, 1990). Harland et al.'s high motivation categories are possibly more rare among 'consumers' of the arts, with 'task-oriented and physiological/therapeutic' arguably implying some kind of physical involvement, while 'self-identity/expression and intrinsic' also suggest a level of commitment to the arts that goes beyond the spectator role.

Further research would need to be done to test these categories on non-participant users of the arts, but where comparisons do exist, it seems that reasons for attending the arts rarely reflect the attitudes associated with highest motivation. Respondents in London (Mass Observation, 1990), Birmingham (Harris Research Centre, 1993a), Ireland (Moore, 1997) and Scotland (System Three, 1998) all echoed the view that the arts are princi-pally seen as entertainment, with the main criteria for a good night out being value for money and an enjoyable social event. Too often, it seems, the arts are considered unable to provide this, with the result that young people may not have the opportunity to develop the highly positive perceptions of the arts that could result in enhanced motivation.

There is some discrepancy among the available research as to whether it is physical or psychological barriers that have the greatest effect on non-attenders, with considerable evidence that high levels of support exist even where participation is rare. Research for the Scottish Arts Council has per-haps gone furthest in investigating attitudes to the arts, with 96 per cent of the 1500 respondents agreeing with the given statement that 'arts and cultural activities give a lot of pleasure to many people' (System Three, 1998). Subjects in Social Classes A and B were most likely to agree that 'artists, writers and performers are important people who contribute to society', with a slight rural bias towards agreement that 'central government has a responsibility to support arts and culture'. Unfortunately for our current purposes, these results are not presented according to age, and, in any case, only 10 per cent of respondents were aged 18–24 and could be said to reflect the 'youth' perspective.

The African-Caribbean and Asian subjects interviewed in Birmingham by the Harris Research Centre (1993a) were aged between 21 and 35 years, and therefore closer to the target age group, but their strong sense of cultural identity has a more powerful defining role in their responses. While physical barriers, such as cost, travel and childcare feature prominently in discussion, the perceived cultural and social irrelevance of the arts is also significant (Harris Research Centre, 1993a). While cautious of the separa-tion that a 'Black Arts Festival' might engender, respondents spoke of being conscious of their minority status in the average arts venue audience, lead-ing the researchers to conclude that 'it is the feeling of alienation which seems to form the greatest barrier'. Echoing the earlier barrier types of 'lack of relevance and comfortability', many of the subjects interviewed made a clear distinction between 'entertainment', which was sometimes expensive but included the whole family, and 'arts', which had little connection with everyday life.

Feelings of alienation from the arts were also reported in Moore's (1997) study in Ireland of people living in poverty, demonstrated in the fact that they were unlikely to attend even those events which were free. Moore identified five types of barrier: financial, practical, social, physical and cultural, and observed that the social and cultural barriers were the most difficult to remove. Like the Asian and African-Caribbean respondents in the Harris Research Centre study (1993a), Moore's subjects felt uncomfortable with 'the culture and assumptions of those who present the art form', perceiving the arts as being inaccessible and therefore irrelevant.

The National Campaign for the Arts (1999) claims that non-attenders 'offer the excuse of cost and inconvenience to mask a more deep-seated discomfort with the arts'. Conversely, the Northern Arts Marketing Company (AMCo, 1993) reported that barriers to attendance are more often actual than perceived. Clearly, these organisations have specific agendas that may affect their presentation of results, but it is certainly the case that physical barriers are often mentioned, especially by those people who profess a high level of interest in the arts. Cost, not just of tickets but of associated expenses such as travel and childcare, emerges frequently as a barrier to attendance, although the majority of those who had attended in the past reported getting value-for-money that was equal to or better than they had expected (System Three, 1998). The Mass Observation researchers argue that the cost of events needs to be put in perspective, stating that the actual expense of an evening at a cultural venue is often no greater than that of other activities that are more frequently pursued. However, the element of risk involved in spending money on an arts event is part of this perception, with 60 per cent of the London non-attenders stating that they did not like going to see things they did not know much about.

The Northern Arts Marketing Company experimented with eliminating the difficulties of cost by offering free tickets to selected local events to infrequent arts attenders in social classes C1 and C2. The majority of those who attended as a result of the scheme enjoyed their visit, with the main hindrance to full enjoyment proving to be uncomfortable seats. Most claimed that they would go to the theatre again if the physical barriers of cost and access were removed, and showed very mainstream tastes in their proposed repertoire, 77 per cent favouring comedies, with thrillers, musicals and jazz/folk/rock/pop concerts attracting 74 per cent each. Follow-up telephone interviews revealed that while some respondents were more aware of the arts and had made subsequent visits to arts venues, others were still being prevented by the same barriers of cost, transport and lack of time. This mirrors the concerns of the NCA that short-term initiatives, such as free or cheap tickets, have little long-term effect: 'low prices as a "one-off" gimmick cannot be the basis for a relationship with an audience for whom price is a genuine obstacle to participation'.

Cost is not the only physical barrier to emerge across the available research studies, with transport, availability of information, lack of time and having no one to go with also frequently cited. The problem of access arises in the Mass Observation study (1990), with female, elderly and disabled people most likely to 'feel unsafe on public transport' in London. Elsewhere, the lack of available transport is more of a problem, and Moore (1997) and AMCo (1993) note that where economically disadvantaged groups use public transport rather than having their own car, the problems of attending arts venues are compounded.

Much of the available research on audience attitudes relates to the theatre, but the Harris Research Centre (1993b) and Research Surveys of Great Britain (1994) have carried out investigations of audience perceptions at orchestral concerts. The quantitative study (RSGB, 1994) focused particularly on those people who had expressed some interest in classical music, but were unlikely to attend live concerts, with 16–24 year olds forming 10 per cent of the total sample. The familiar considerations of cost, travel, and fear of the unknown emerged as barriers to attendance, with 'the desire to learn' featuring as an attitude apparently specific to this genre; 'the need for more complete information about pieces and performances was a consistent theme'. Interest in classical music rose through the age groups, with 12 per cent of the 16–34 age group claiming to be 'very interested', in comparison with 26 per cent of 35–54 year olds, and 36 per cent of the 55+ group. Non-attenders, in particular, were likely to see orchestral concerts as being special occasions, holding positive perceptions but not considering concerts to be places to go frequently. It seems that the mystique surrounding large-scale classical music performances has a dual effect, increasing the perceived importance of events, while acting as a barrier to attendance for a significant potential audience.

The Harris Research Centre's (1993b) qualitative research offers comparable results, although here all participants were aged 25–55. Some insight into the listening habits of younger people is still forthcoming, with many respondents citing parental or school influence on their adult listening habits. Constructing a typology of listeners from their group discussions, the researchers suggest that the younger respondents tended to be either 'light listeners', who enjoyed popular classics but usually as a displacement activity, or 'active listeners', who were developing more committed listening habits and were a little more likely to attend concerts. 'Committed listeners', with an extensive repertoire and regular concert attendance, tended to be in the older age groups. Many respondents referred to pleasurable listening experiences as children, and were now continuing that cycle with their own children, either gaining a new interest as a result of a child's involvement with a youth orchestra, or deliberately cultivating enjoyment of music by taking their children to orchestral concerts. As in the Harris Research Centre's (1993a) Birmingham study, the influence of family behaviour and attitudes is shown to be significant in developing audience enjoyment for young people and their parents.

Like the RSGB respondents, the Harris Research Centre's subjects were put off by the sense of occasion attached to concert-going: 'concerts seemed to require a different etiquette, often appearing formal and reflecting elitism'. Interestingly, however, a preference was expressed for the orchestra to be in evening dress, suggesting that attempts to create a friendlier atmosphere by relaxing such conventions are unlikely to be successful. Pre- and post-concert activities were seen by respondents as being more effective in reducing formality. All members of the sample had expressed an interest in classical music that was usually demonstrated by listening to recordings and broadcasts at home, with an enjoyment of live recordings and transmissions suggesting that the feeling that 'someone is playing that instrument now' adds a certain excitement. Others expressed a preference for edited recordings, finding the audience presence intrusive rather than beneficial. This ambiguity was carried over into attitudes to concerts, with respondents perceiving more sense of purpose in going to the theatre, when the performance is unlikely to be available elsewhere.

While young people agreed with the general population that cost was important, they were more likely to list lack of time and lack of opportunity as being significant factors in their low participation rates (Harland and Kinder, 1995). The *Youth Audience Research Report* (ACE, 1994) goes some way towards exploring the physical barriers that particularly affect young people, noting that cost was the reason given by around half the respondents for infrequent attendance, with lack of time (32 per cent) a little way behind. The AMCo researchers noted that with almost one-third of respondents claiming to be too busy to attend cultural organisations, the success of any marketing incentives is by no means guaranteed. To remove one physical barrier may merely be to divert attention to another, and thus simultaneous strategies may be needed to address the 'deep-seated discomfort' that the NCA identifies.

Given the constraints under which they work, museums and galleries increasingly appear to be consulting youth workers, as well as young people and children themselves, on the attitudes and decision-making of young visitors (Verge, 1994; Marwick, 1994). Tilley (1997), Selwood et al. (1995) and Fowle's (1997) findings suggest that, in general, young people who are not attenders merely felt that museums would hold nothing of interest for them. Like other non-attenders young people are likely to regard such institutions as establishment, and their displays as 'static' (Selwood et al.). Although first-time visitors expected art museums to be dull, in the event they found that they weren't 'as boring as you might think'. However, they wanted to be made to feel welcome, they wanted the cafés to be cheaper, and they wanted better signs and orientation: 'the art museum is like a maze'. They also called for better displays and presentation: 'as you go upstairs it's all brown – yuk', and less text-based information. Labels were criticised as being 'old and falling apart – it looks as though the museum doesn't care much', and as being poorly placed – 'too high'. Like other visitors they wanted a greater degree of comfort – 'it's a shame there's nowhere to sit down and talk about exhibits'. Other requirements included music in the galleries, more information in the form of 'statements from artists' and 'audio-guides made by young people'. They also wanted access to the people involved – 'to meet artists' and 'other people working on the museum' (Fowle, 1997; Tilley, 1997).

Using group discussions with students and young employees aged 15–19, MAX (Marketing the Arts in Oxfordshire, 1998) has carried out further research into young people's attitudes. Like Willis (1990), they emphasise the stages of maturity experienced by teenagers, charting the development from group security through individuality to the emergence of an adult role. Arts initiatives, they claim, need to be responsive to these stages, planning group events for 16–17 year olds, while emphasising independent adult activities for those over 17. Barriers included the problems of physical access and prohibitive expense, as well as negative associations that link the arts primarily with older, middle-class people. Among the respondents involved in the MAX survey, the categories of 'dabblers', who enjoy occasional arts events, 'enthusiasts', who will often have an established participatory relationship with the arts, and 'drag alongs', who have little natural affinity with the arts, emerge along with the 'embarrassed' group who see the arts as 'uncool' but have a degree of potential interest. Viewing these sub-sections alongside the proposed stages of maturity begins to create a realistically complex picture of young people's perceptions, highlighting the fact that a simplistic or generalised approach to increasing access is unlikely to be successful.

MAX presents a commentary rather than clear evidence, making it difficult to compare data with other published studies. Nevertheless, the factors of perceived irrelevance and stuffiness appear more often than is typical, with respondents calling for events that are 'more appealing and related to youth culture'. Accordingly, the young people consulted were receptive to the ideas of one-off arts events organised by or for them. Longitudinal studies of the effects of these and similar projects would be necessary to determine if such 'youth-focused' events led to more long-term shifts in attitude. Such studies have recently been called for by the DCMS (GB. DCMS, 1999b).

Clearly, the mixture of psychological and physical factors associated with infrequent attendance at cultural venues makes the development of strategies for increasing access a complex task. Cost is obviously a factor, but occasional free or discounted tickets do not remove the problem in the long term (NCA, 1999), and do little to tackle the perception of the arts as being inaccessible in more general terms. Arts organisations and funding bodies have been called upon to make the changes necessary to attract more young people, but it is evident that attitudes to the arts are formed in a wider context, among family, friends and teachers. The next section will open up discussion of the role that can be played by the influential figures in young people's lives, as well as by the arts organisations themselves.

2.4 THE INFLUENCE OF SCHOOLS, FAMILIES AND CULTURAL ORGANISATIONS/VENUES

2.4.1 Schools

Several of the studies considered here raise questions about the role of schools in increasing awareness of the arts in preparation for wider and longer-term cultural involvement. For example, Moore's (1997) economically disadvantaged respondents in Ireland claimed a significant role for teachers, with 24 per cent suggesting there had been an improvement in arts education since their own schooldays. On the other hand, school can engender negative attitudes to the arts, and it is interesting to note that among Harland et al.'s (1995) young subjects, it was the under-17 year old school pupils who felt 'most in need of moral support, encouragement and appreciation in the arts'. Nonetheless, 14 per cent of those respondents cited a secondary arts teacher as being the single most important factor in 'turning them on' to the arts, the highest result where the young people could recall such an effect. The responsibility of arts teachers' roles is emphasised further when they also emerged as the single biggest 'turn off' factor, with a slightly lower result of nine per cent nominating them as a negative influence.

There is no doubt that the picture is a complex one, and that schools can have negative, as well as positive, effects on young people's attitudes to attending cultural venues. Most importantly, it cannot be assumed that all school organised visits to cultural venues are automatically of benefit in encouraging young people to attend in the future. O'Brien's (1996) MORI survey, for example, showed that of those visiting arts festivals, galleries and opera (both in and out of school), only about half enjoyed their visit. Thus, a crucial research question emerges: under what conditions do teachers, along with the cultural experience itself, increase young people's motivation to attend similar venues again?

Unfortunately, the review found little research that had addressed this issue. By way of illustration, little research was identified on the level of school provision in encouraging engagement in cultural venues or on the effects of school visits to cultural venues, beyond such observations as that behaviour in galleries varies according to whom visitors are accompanied by (McManus, 1987) and sporadic accounts of young people's own reflections:

I think that teachers don't think art is important so they don't want to cover for visits to art galleries. They don't think it's work ...
(Selwood et al., 1995: 45)

Most reports on collaborations between schools and museums are evaluations of particular projects (GB. HMI, 1991; Bull, 1993), predominantly in terms of their contributions to student learning in school subjects – for instance, Xanthoudaki (1998) studied the role of museum and gallery educational programmes in furthering the goals of classroom art education.

Increasing access to cultural organisations is not strictly part of schools' remit, but the ability to participate in an audience role is widely recognised as being an important part of learning in the arts:

If pupils are to respond discerningly as members of an audience, they will need to develop a critical vocabulary which can be applied to professional productions in and out of school as well as to their own work and that of their peers.
(ACGB, 1992:5)

The Arts Council's comments on drama are equally applicable to other art forms, and are consistent with the views of OFSTED inspectors who praise efforts to make pupils 'more informed consumers of music' (OFSTED, 1998) and to 'enhance observation and critical skills' in dance. Arguably, it is more a question of whether schools are helping young people apply critical faculties through leisure-time attendance at cultural venues, since the National Curriculum includes a critical studies element in most art forms. The NCA go so far as to state that 'the arts entitlement should include the right to learn from artists in residence at school and to make visits to the arts as part of school activity' (NCA, 1998). Rogers (1995b), too, sees regular visits to a wide variety of arts venues as being an essential part of arts education for every pupil. Hopes of establishing visits to cultural organisations within the curriculum may seem overly optimistic, but the proposals highlight the fact that school trips to arts venues are increasingly expensive, and so run the risk of excluding those people who are also least likely to be arts consumers outside school.

Ambivalent attitudes to the importance of attending cultural organisations are evident in Ross and Kamba's (1997) study of the arts in five English secondary schools. The arts teachers were initially asked why they teach the arts, and the five statements they were given to place in rank order included 'so that my students may become literate arts "consumers" – which means investing in and taking pleasure in artistic experiences'. For music teachers, this reason was given equal first ranking with 'to promote the development of my students' personal qualities', while in art and drama it was seen as less important, although all subject teachers gave it priority over the currently and strategically popular, 'way of supporting learning in other subjects'.

The alternative to taking young people to cultural organisations is to bring the performances to them. These contributions to the arts experiences of young people have scope for reducing perceptions of the arts as élitist and irrelevant, and therefore of overcoming the barriers that could prevent regular attendance later. Sharp and Dust (1997) emphasise the benefits for pupils, suggesting that the role models and opportunities offered by visiting artists can act as 'a catalyst for pupils being more open about their own interests in the arts'.

With 74 per cent of the 18–34 year olds in the Mass Observation study (1990) stating that 'making the arts fun at school' would help to generate positive attitudes, it is clear that school is widely perceived as having an important role to play. The researchers note however that 'participation in art classes may not lead to cross-over into spectation', emphasising, perhaps, that such cross-over needs to be deliberately addressed, and not merely left to happen by chance. In general, the potential connections and continuities between school-based education in the arts and engagement in cultural organisations appear to have been surprisingly neglected in the research literature. This may have perpetuated a divide between 'creative' activities that happen in schools, which often operate as 'closed societies' (CGF, 1982), and 'consumer' opportunities beyond the school walls or later in life.

Reflecting arts organisations' heavy emphasis on working with schools, rather fewer museum and gallery projects appear to be targeted at young people outside the formal education sector. However, some institutions seek to attract this group through partnerships with the youth service, as a way of extending take-up. Indeed, some projects come into being as a result of contacts which already exist between gallery staff and youth workers (Selwood et al., 1995). Furthermore, they are often tailored according to youth workers' representations of the 'needs' of their young people. Nevertheless, it appears that visual arts organisations in England are less likely to target the youth service than most other types of arts organisation (Hogarth et al., 1997). There are, of course, exceptions, but generally the research literature does suggest that youth agencies are a comparatively under-used support system in terms of widening young people's attendance at cultural venues.

2.4.2 Family and friends

Also significant in the shaping of young people's attitudes towards cultural organisations is their family background, with parents playing an important role in influencing perceptions (O'Brien, 1996). Moreover, there is North American evidence that, for the museum sector at least, families impart a much greater influence in attendance behaviour than schools:

> ... 60 per cent of regular museum-goers said that their interest in museums had been shaped by a family member, against only 3 per cent who credited school field trips. (Wolins, 1989)

While these findings may not necessarily hold true for the UK, several of the children interviewed for the recent Tate Gallery visitor audit suggested that they preferred visiting with their families than with school. This often pertained to the activities that they were obliged to carry out as part of the schools visit:

> *Sometimes I don't like the activity things because you have quizzes before you do something interesting. I was quizzed about the pictures and I didn't know the answers. So, it takes ages before you can do something you want to do.*
> (Selwood with Traynor, 1998:54)

Despite acknowledging that families should be encouraged to visit, Anderson (1997) found that in the UK relatively few museums and galleries make special provision for them. His survey of 566 museums in the UK found that 32 per cent provided events for families and that 26 per cent provided trails and other resources for families.

A major disadvantage for museums is their image as educational institutions (Prentice, 1994). It has been suggested that less educated parents feel that they may not meet the challenge of interpreting the collections to their children. Rather than face embarrassment, these parents will avoid leisure places they think will be too intellectually challenging. It may be, as Wood (1990) suggests, that museums are 'relying on parents to supply or interpret knowledge of displays to children', and that they may not be 'encouraging and helping them to do so' sufficiently. More recent research carried out in England focuses on the need for parents' own enthusiasm (Harris Qualitative, 1997). Non-attending parents are likely to refer to any number of barriers that inhibit their visiting, including lack of time, children's behaviour, concern about the best value for money.

Similar findings on the influence of families in attending other cultural venues were evident. Adult respondents in the Mass Observation survey (1990) saw childhood experiences as influential in shaping attitudes, saying that 'unless you're brought up in those sorts of circles, you're not educated to go and listen to the opera or go and watch ballet'. The Harris Research Centre (1993a) noticed the effect of mothers, finding that 'Asian females were usually the dominant factor in the decision-making process', and also observing that the Asian respondents tended to do things as a family, rather than with a partner. While this restricted arts attendance to a certain extent, because of the greater cost, it also meant that the Asian women were supportive of initiatives that increased their children's cultural opportunities.

Further evidence can be found in Harland et al. (1995), where many respondents report a 'family osmosis' effect in their growing interest in the arts, with females and high educational attainers most likely to cite their parents, particularly mothers, as a significant influence. This was a particular trait of middle class families: twice as many interviewees from professional families described being 'turned on to' the arts by their mothers than those from other social backgrounds. Parents were much more rarely seen as a 'turn off'.

The influence of friends and peers on arts consumption is also significant, most noticeably for its detrimental effects, when 'peer pressure' acts to reinforce negative perceptions of the arts (MAX, 1998). Harland et al. (1995) also found that perceived dissonance with the self or group identity, and anticipation of negative reactions from others formed a barrier to attendance. This social dimension to arts consumption is supported by evidence from the Mass Observation (1990) study, where 47 per cent of respondents in the lower socio-economic groups gave 'my friends tend not to go' as a reason for infrequent arts attendance.

Gathering data on the effects of peers and family is a particularly sensitive area, and it is difficult to form conclusions from existing evidence. Generally speaking, it seems true to say that families and friends have the potential to be a significant force in shaping attitudes and affecting behaviour. Where a supportive family environment exists, interest in the arts can be fostered, but the effects of apathy or antipathy on the part of relatives and friends must also be taken into account.

2.4.3 Cultural venues

Cultural venues generally recognise that it is in their interests to secure the support and custom of the youth audience, fostering patterns of attendance that could have a lifetime effect. The Arts Council, for example, states that 'high-quality, innovative educational work should be an intrinsic part of every funded arts organisation's programmes' (ACE, 1997), and has pledged to disseminate good practice and support new initiatives. Strategies to increase accessibility have been reviewed by the NCA (1999) and by AMCo (1993), with both emphasising that cultural venues will have to instigate changes to overcome the barriers that affect non-attenders. The NCA acknowledges that existing marketing strategies are most likely to increase attendance among those who are already going to performances and exhibitions, but that 'the largest and by far the hardest group to reach is that which has little or no developed interest'. Encouragingly, the NCA note that schemes such as 'Pay as You Please' projects, where audience members suggest their own ticket prices, do not result in a loss of revenue for the venue, as increased attendance and bar sales compensate for cheaper seats (1999). Alongside this, they emphasise the importance of including work of the highest quality in such schemes, rather than using them to fill 'the hard to sell shows and the least popular evenings or seats'. Similar strategies are suggested by AMCo, who stress that first time visitors need encouraging to return. Altering performance times, to offer daytime or early evening shows, could go some way towards easing the difficulties of childcare and travel arrangements, so overcoming the practical barriers described by many respondents.

With 'lack of information' cited by many respondents as a reason for infrequent attendance (Mass Observation, 1990), the advertising of any initiatives aimed at irregular visitors needs careful thought. Respondents in the Harris Research Centre (1993a) study saw publicity for arts events as being sparse, and found that the predominant use of English reinforced the perception that the arts were not for minority groups. The use of local radio and word of mouth recommendations were found to be most influential among Asian and African-Caribbean respondents, whereas the System Three (1998) research found leaflets through doors to be the most popular advertising strategy. AMCo (1993) reported a high percentage of people gathering arts listings information from newspapers (79 per cent), leaflets (71 per cent) and posters (83 per cent), with the latter two noticed at libraries, shops and restaurants, as well as at the arts venues themselves.

Evidence from the museum sector suggests that the quality of the experience gained through attendance is every bit as important as marketing strategies in winning over young people and family groups. The kind of exhibits which are observed to capture families' attention tend to be interactive, with audio-visual components (Beer, 1987). Blud (1990a; 1990b) found that different exhibits stimulate different kinds of interaction, and that interactive exhibits may be successful in stimulating constructive discussion between adults and children. Attributes deemed essential to making family visits desirable and successful include the fulfilment of certain leisure criteria, satisfying child-centred interests, and providing something for the family to do together (Hood, 1989). It has been suggested that families want opportunities to interact socially and participate actively in things, rather than opportunities to learn or do something 'worthwhile' with their leisure time (Yerk, 1984). Entertainment is regarded as a key element.

The literature suggests that the entirety of the museum visit is important to families, not just the content of an exhibition or the comprehensibility of the labels, but the ease of getting around, levels of comfort, and other services provided. In short, families will go to places where they expect to feel welcome, comfortable and rewarded. They return to those which meet their expectations and where they are satisfied with the total experience.

In recent years, many museums and galleries have recognised the poor representation of young people among their visitors and have devised various projects to attract them (Mathers, 1996). The ways in which museums and galleries seek to attract young people include: targeted programming and marketing strategies; involving them in advisory groups and exhibition curation to attract their peers, and in helping to develop the quality of young visitors' experience to encourage return visits; installing multi-media interpretive materials; and providing them with opportunities to develop their skills and work with artists. As implied, these initiatives are often based on the principle of encouraging young people to participate actively in some way (Selwood et al., 1995; Rider and Illingworth, 1997; Tilley, 1997).

Several studies point to the importance of allowing young people to meet performers and others working in arts venues. The Arts Council, in their discussions of dance (ACGB, 1993) and drama (ACGB, 1992) emphasise the opportunities for interacting with professional performers and gaining knowledge of how arts venues operate. The Community Development Foundation (1992) suggest that similar opportunities could be provided outside school, in a bid to overcome the 'cultural myopia' that threatens to undermine the arts.

In short, it seems that cultural venues have much to offer education, community work and young people in general, with successful partnerships likely to be one of the most effective ways of challenging the psychological barriers that surround arts attendance. So often, the research literature signals that arts education and community initiatives are based on participatory approaches (Whitfield, 1991), suggesting perhaps that more attention could be given to ways of increasing young people's skills and enjoyment as audience members. Again, longitudinal research would be helpful in tracing the changing perceptions of the young people involved, and in monitoring the extent to which practical involvement in arts venues, at whatever level, affect long-term attendance patterns. After the following conclusion, Chapter 3 takes a closer look at some of the main types of initiatives being used to increase young people's attendance at cultural venues.

2.5 CONCLUSION

The research evidence shows that attendance at cultural venues declines as children progress through their teens. The mid-teens appear to be associated with particularly low levels of audience involvement, with some evidence of higher rates among young people in their early twenties. Generally, males and young people from semi-skilled or unskilled backgrounds were more likely to be non-attenders than girls or middle class teenagers. Parental influence was found to be an important factor in encouraging involvement.

One possible interpretation of these findings is that attendance during the early teens is higher due to the perceived acceptability of the image of attending such venues as part of the family. As children mature into the mid-teens, increased desires for independence, peer group influences and new forms of social interaction, along with the pressures of examinations, make it less acceptable to attend cultural venues with parents. In the early twenties, often with the demands and financial constraints of tertiary education behind them, more young people, especially those who have inherited cultural capital, re-engage and re-define them as part of their own emerging independent life style, meanings and social network.

The review found very little evidence on the school's contribution to encouraging applied and independent engagement with cultural venues. What was available was, at best, ambivalent: schools could help turn young people on to the arts, but they could also turn them off. Considering the available evidence on the reasons why some young people are motivated to attend cultural venues, it may well be the case that more schools could support pupils' audience-based engagement in the arts explicitly for their 'entertainment' value. Many respondents in the various studies appeared to be saying that, in the first instance at least, attendance at the kind of cultural venues discussed here needed to offer an enjoyable experience rather than more 'school work'. Additionally, the tentative conclusion reached by Harland et al. (1995) that change through dramatic conversions experienced at single arts events (Hargreaves, 1983) is less common than sustained support from significant others who mediate the arts over a period of time suggests that the quality of any facilitating role provided by teachers, youth leaders and arts workers is every bit as important as the experience itself. From this perspective, it is pertinent to ask whether an appropriate pedagogy and curriculum for equipping young people with the necessary knowledge, skills and attitudes to enable them to access cultural venues remains to be developed.

To this end, research into effective school-based strategies for developing the audience role could be timely and informative. The review also demonstrated that more investigations into the patterns of young people's attendance at cultural venues are required, as well as more longer-term evaluations of the impact on young people of initiatives to promote wider youth access to cultural venues.

Increasing young people's access to cultural organisations necessitates the overcoming of physical barriers, such as cost, travel and lack of time, and psychological barriers, including perceptions that the arts are irrelevant or culturally exclusive. Of these, the psychological barriers are likely to be more deep-seated. Moreover, the research evidence suggested that removing barriers may be a necessary but not a sufficient condition of increasing youth access to the arts: positive incentives seem to be essential as well. Valuing the role of the audience, not just as a commercial factor, but as an essential part of the arts experience, would seem to be a key factor in increasing levels of cultural inclusion.

Throughout the literature, there is an apparent need to strengthen perceptions of the importance of education for the audience role, and perhaps shed the sense of inferiority that occurs in much of the discourse (DNH, 1996; GB. DfEE. DCMS. NACCCE, 1999). Research reports, policy documents and curriculum guidelines tend to short-change the development of the audience role in general and the fostering of the habit of attending cultural venues in particular. As a common entitlement for all children, a formal curriculum statement requiring schools to ensure that every pupil visits a theatre, a gallery, a museum, a music and a dance performance during primary and secondary phases would be one way of giving this aspect of arts education greater status. Obviously, by itself this entitlement could not be guaranteed to deliver the desired outcomes. To stand any chance of building positive attitudes towards cultural inclusion, such a policy would need to be adequately resourced and, most importantly, integrated into a wider and longer-term commitment to pedagogies and curricula capable of motivating and empowering young people.

Understandably, very few arts teachers would countenance the replacement of participatory arts activities with a return to 'appreciation' lessons, but O'Neill's (1989) observation that the audience 'can be persuaded but never commanded to participate in the event' is a reminder that listening, viewing, and evaluation skills need to be acquired and applied through nurtured experience and education (Hornbrook, 1991). If they are not, perceptions of the arts as being 'difficult to relate to' (Harris Research Centre, 1993a), 'for other people' (Moore, 1997) or even 'boring, rubbish' (Harland and Kinder, 1995) are likely to be perpetuated.

3 AN ILLUSTRATIVE AUDIT OF RECENT INITIATIVES

Mary Ashworth, John Harland and Sara Selwood

3.1 INTRODUCTION

The audit began by investigating the range of initiatives intended to encourage young people's attendance at cultural venues across the full spectrum of art forms. Bearing the aims of the project in mind, the nature of the marketing and programming strategies deployed by arts organisations to attract 14–18 year olds was subject to particular scrutiny. Preliminary inquiries uncovered a plethora of initiatives and in many cases respondents recommended further contacts. Such prolific variety suggested an emerging patchwork of local and regional initiatives, some already benefiting from lines of mutual communication and support, and the whole offering myriad opportunities for replication, adaptation and innovation.

Although the research focused on initiatives seeking to extend young people's audience attendance at cultural venues, in practice there were very few projects that did not also involve some element of participation for them, either as artists, advisers or impresarios. Given the seemingly inexhaustible number of arts projects for young people recommended by the primary contacts, it became necessary to present the audit as an illustrative, and highly selective, account of initiatives perceived by the organisers to be successful, together with their respective marketing strategies. The choice of initiatives represented was determined by the intention to present what may appear to be significant discernible trends, while at the same time giving some insight into the imaginative possibilities of individual variations. The audit is in no way intended to be evaluative and does not offer judgements on any individual initiatives. For the most part, the audit focuses on arts organisations, though occasionally examples are cited from the museums sector. In accordance with the NFER Code of Practice, all information from respondents is regarded as strictly confidential; individuals and organisations are referred to anonymously throughout.

3.2 METHODOLOGY

In order to ensure as far as possible that the first round of contacts would be appropriate to the aims of the research, arts initiatives which were known from preliminary information to place the emphasis on participation as an end in itself, rather than as a complementary dimension to audience attendance, were deferred for use later in the study, should there be a need for further data.

Data for the audit were collected through telephone discussions with marketing and/or education officers of the respective venues, schemes and organisations. In most cases, the information gathered over the telephone was supplemented by relevant documentation (e.g. publicity material, annual reports, evaluations) subsequently forwarded by post, and any additional clarification was gained by further telephone calls. Once it became apparent that the number of initiatives eligible for investigation was considerably greater than originally anticipated, the number of telephone calls was restricted to those perceived by the first respondents to be directing their energies towards extending young people's attendance at cultural events, and other organisations were contacted by post.

The following discussion attempts to outline the main strategies for marketing the arts to young people aged 14–18 years, as they emerged from the data collected. The marketing strategies themselves are classified according to a typology that evolved during the analysis. This is preceded by a brief account of the relative timescales of the different projects and an outline of the range of initiatives in different art forms, according to the specific groups of young people they aimed to attract. While some analysis may also be included in relation to individual initiatives as they occur within sub-categories, a consideration of some key issues will follow the typology.

Examples of initiatives in discrete art forms will appear under each category. However, it may be a significant finding in itself that, in a number of cases, a multi-media or 'multi-arts' approach was perceived to make an experience more appealing to young people. Several initiatives were directed at young people who were perceived, and assumed to perceive themselves, as socially marginalised or excluded. In this case, the emphasis, in the first instance, was on the therapeutic value of the arts; this multi-faceted approach was frequently referred to as 'holistic', and in some initiatives extended to cover other areas such as health, unemployment or domestic problems.

3.3 TIMESCALE

Very few initiatives operated as isolated one-off events. In most cases they fell into one of two categories: either they were short- to medium-term with long-term aims, or they were 'ongoing'.

3.3.1 Short- to medium-term initiatives with long-term aims
Initiatives in this category were planned to run for a limited duration;

continuation was seen to depend on funding available, and the direction indicated by the success of the current project.

One example where this was applicable concerned an orchestra in the north of England that was currently involved in a major three-year project in an inner-city location. The initiative was aimed at young people with little or no experience of 'culture' or 'the arts'. A highly significant factor had been the 'credibility' acquired through working with youth officers, adults whom young people felt they could trust. The extended duration of the project was seen as essential to allow the orchestra itself time to earn credibility in young people's perceptions.

3.3.2 Ongoing initiatives

Initiatives which could be regarded as continuous, or, in some cases, self-perpetuating, were perceived to be the most successful in sustaining the commitment that results in regular attendance, although in the majority of cases, the role of participation in motivating that attendance must be borne in mind. In this respect, several major national orchestras could attest to the cumulative benefits of well-established and continuing programmes of school and community work.

A major northern art gallery started a new advisory group five years ago which involved young people aged between 14 and 25 working with gallery staff on a programme of activities for their peers. Significantly, 'consultation over an extended period of time' was perceived to have played a vital role in allowing the gallery 'to fine-tune its services for young people'.

As stated at the beginning of this section, very few of the initiatives under scrutiny operated as isolated one-off events. According to individuals working with young people in successful long-term initiatives, it had been the extended duration of the project that had enabled staff to adapt the programme in response to emerging needs expressed by young people themselves. It was felt that a long-term impact was much more likely to occur if participants were allowed to 'colonise' (Willis, 1990) a venue or an art form. Young people need time, to develop an interest, to gain the confidence to offer their own ideas and to realise them in a way which makes the venue or the art form more appealing to themselves and their peers. In practical terms, this requires long-term funding.

3.4 NATURE OF TARGET AUDIENCE

A considerable number of initiatives for 14–18 year olds appeared to concentrate on the 'captive audience' available in schools, with the dual benefits of readymade structures for planning, and experienced teachers familiar with both the ethos of the particular school and the young people themselves, both as groups and individuals. However, at the same time, bearing in mind that it may be difficult to introduce secondary pupils to more challenging cultural experiences for which their earlier schooling has not prepared them, a number of respondents reported that they were directing most of their educational activities at the primary age group.

It was generally agreed that young people outside school are more elusive, especially those who are not in contact with the local youth service. The following sub-categories illustrate the ways in which appropriately tailored initiatives are currently directing their energies towards designated groups of young people both in and out of school with some perceived success.

3.4.1 Young people in school

As already stated, it may be worth remembering that schools can be 'closed societies' (CGF, 1982). A currently unknown number of young people may 'compartmentalise' their arts experiences in school, to the extent that they bear little relation to what they perceive to be available to them in the world outside. Nevertheless, diverse and well-established initiatives currently operate between arts organisations and school. In the interests of brevity, as with initiatives operating elsewhere, one or two examples must speak for the rest.

One of two schemes recently developed by the DfEE, to encourage the relationship between schools, museums and galleries, provides £140,000 for 17 'study support projects' to devise learning opportunities for young people out of school hours (GB. DfEE, 1998). Of those, nine projects embrace 14–18 year olds.

A music institution with a deliberately eclectic approach creates opportunities for young people to develop personal skills and interests in different genres. They target 'not the top students but the tier below, the kids who are keen and committed but maybe their parents can't get them to Saturday music school, or maybe they're rock musicians for whom development is not very formalised'.

3.4.2 Young people out of school

As one arts worker observed, contact with this group, in both rural and urban areas, can be more difficult to establish and sustain because the network of contacts is less formalised. The informality and flexibility of local youth services was highly valued in this respect, as was their 'credibility' with young people – although there is evidence that the majority of young people attending youth clubs are 16 years old or under, so the youth service may only provide alternative access to school-aged teenagers rather than to those of post-compulsory schooling age (Harland et al., 1995). Nevertheless, many arts organisations affirmed that they rely on the youth service for building a bridge between themselves and young people out of school.

A notable example concerns a major symphony orchestra said to be 'different from many other orchestras', because it avoids being 'heavily school-based'. The orchestra's education officer attributed the success of out of school activities to the policy of approaching young people through youth clubs, working 'organically' and building on existing contacts with no set formula.

Elsewhere, outreach activity involved staff from a regional theatre approaching young people informally outside the theatre in order to promote a 'multi-layered experience' in the theatre foyer, with video screens, a party on the opening night and monitors giving access to the Internet. This had been deliberately designed to appeal to young people familiar with multi-media events in their local pubs and clubs.

In some venues a 'holistic approach' created a variety of services for young people alongside a wide range of arts opportunities in which they were free to participate. In an urban location in the south-east, for example, a Young People's Centre had recently been opened after intensive consultation with younger residents in particular. It offered many opportunities for 14–18s, some but not all of which were arts-oriented.

According to the instigators of all initiatives recorded here for young people out of school, the most effective way to appeal to them was through an informal and versatile approach, which communicated an acceptance of current youth culture. Scrupulous consultation and open access were deemed to be of paramount importance.

3.4.3 Young people both in and out of school

Some cultural organisations market their events to young people both in and out of school.

One major symphony orchestra invites pupils in specific age groups. In order to ensure an appropriate programme, they provide a tape and teacher's pack and hold INSET sessions to arrange preliminary classwork. The orchestra reaches young people out of school through family concerts.

An art gallery initiative to create a young people's advisory group selected members according to the following criteria:

i. they had to be 14–25 years old;
ii. they had to live in the gallery's locality; and
iii. they had to have had previous contact with the gallery.

This strategy gave the gallery access to those young people in and out of school who were seen to offer a level of interest and commitment.

As observed earlier on, young people in school are initially easier to reach than those out of school, who require a much more flexible approach. Young people's accessibility in a school setting may imply greater compliance. Whether this has any bearing on their willingness to experiment with something unfamiliar remains to be determined.

3.4.4 Young people from ethnic minorities

During the first half of 1999, a series of music-based initiatives was deliberately aimed at groups of young people whose cultural interests were seen to be neglected. This series included a succession of African and Caribbean carnival events in large indoor venues in four provincial cities. At about the same time, an Asian music/multi-media event toured clubs around the country, appearing in a variety of arts-based venues and mainstream clubs. A pilot television programme was also produced; this featured black club culture and was broadcast on a student television network.

A northern arts marketing organisation recently supported local theatres in encouraging young Asians to attend mainstream venues through the 'Test Drive the Arts' scheme. In this case, ten young Asians were recruited through focus groups to act as 'arts ambassadors' and recruit ten people each from among their friends. The one hundred young Asians who attended the performance have subsequently thus become potential audience members.

Specific projects aimed at young people in ethnic minorities were not conspicuous among the clusters of initiatives uncovered by this study. Perhaps this is a significant finding in itself. It may highlight the need for special sensitivity: firstly, in relation to initiatives which positively discriminate in this way, and secondly, in relation to how such young people may feel about the recognition of their own culture, about any possible sense of isolation because their culture is discrete, and also about being included in cultural events for young people which are not ethnically specific. It would be very interesting to learn how they would define an acceptable version of the two-way culture (Richey, 1996) referred to in the introduction.

3.4.5 Disaffected or marginalised young people

A number of initiatives were aimed at disaffected young people. Staff at a city art gallery were currently working with local secondary school pupils and young offenders to explore interpretations of the gallery's current exhibition relating to the millennium. This was one of five new school/gallery projects linking into the annual Gallery Week.

A regional arts board (RAB) had recently launched an initiative that ran eight separate projects through a specialist youth arts agency. The aim of the initiative was 'to support the extension of specialist youth arts work for young people at risk, to demonstrate the preventative benefits of the arts and to improve provision for young people in a range of disadvantaged situations and locations'. One of these projects was operating in both urban and rural areas. The inner-city strand was directed at 12–18 year olds; this project was 'site-specific', with mobile facilities for studio-style music, and activities were supported by both professional artists and youth workers. Participants included young offenders, excluded school pupils, unemployed young people and others excluded from mainstream provision, and a young people's forum ensured their views were taken into account at every stage of development. The rural version, with 13–19 year olds, was taking the form of outreach work, covering participation in a variety of art forms in relatively isolated communities.

3.4.6 Disabled young people

A number of organisations were directing their attention towards young disabled people. One of the orchestras in the audit, for example, worked with the visually impaired services to increase partially sighted and blind young people's exposure to symphonic and creative music. Another liaised with music therapists on concerts and workshops for children with special needs.

Elsewhere a RAB co-ordinated two projects for young people with or without disabilities. The first involved building more art forms into an existing dance group. Funding for the second supported a performing arts agency in nurturing a sense of empowerment and self-determination in young people of all abilities through specific cultural and vocational learning opportunities.

Projects for disabled young people seemed to be mainly participatory for the same therapeutic reasons as those aimed at disaffected, marginalised individuals: participation was valued for generating self-confidence and a sense of belonging.

3.4.7 Gender-specific initiatives

Because there was relatively little evidence of gender-specific initiatives, the number of boys' dance projects was somewhat conspicuous. A current project, funded by A4E, and deemed by the respondents to be very successful, was for boys in schools. Drawing on the affinities between dance and football skills, their repertoire communicated the sheer exuberance of physical expression through music relevant to young people's own culture.

The only initiative that appeared to be catering specifically for girls was a production at a youth theatre exploring the experiences of teenage mothers. Girls from the local community participated in workshops and in the performance, in an effort to bring a challenging and highly 'relevant' issue, out into the open.

The preceding discussion offers some insight into initiatives across a range of art forms that attract the attention of young people by creating opportunities for specific target groups. However, as a significant number of respondents averred, unless arts organisations bear young people's own priorities and preconceptions in mind when they devise their programmes and marketing strategies, they risk losing their appeal for a potential teenage audience.

3.5 MARKETING STRATEGIES

All organisations and venues in the audit were involved in marketing their events and activities, but they varied considerably in the degree to which they concentrated their resources on overcoming the 'physical' or the 'psychological' barriers to attendance, as identified in the preceding chapter. The marketing strategies which emerged from the data could be seen to range along a continuum, highlighting to varying degrees the *extrinsic* or *intrinsic* appeal of an event or venue as set out below.

The extrinsic appeal of a cultural event or experience

i.   The appeal of material incentives (overcoming physical barriers)
     Ticket schemes and discounts
     Free transport
ii. The appeal of the marketing medium (overcoming psychological barriers)
     Using a communication system appealing and familiar to young people
     Marketing through mediators with street credibility
     Marketing the event in terms of young people's own culture
     Linguistic credibility – through publicity
     *   – in presenting/interpreting the event*
     Transforming the experience of a traditional mainstream venue
     Creating new venues designed specifically for youth arts
     Transferring the event to an alternative venue oriented to youth culture
     The flexibility and informality of mobile arts facilities

The intrinsic appeal of the cultural event or experience

i.   Relevance of the art form to young people's own culture (overcoming psychological barriers)
     The cultural hybrid
     Tailoring an event to accommodate young people's spectating habits
ii. Relevance of the content to young people's interests and concerns (overcoming psychological barriers)
     'Real-life' relevance (e.g. plays about bullying, teenage mothers)
     Humorous perspectives

'Extrinsic' appeal here refers to external factors such as the marketing medium, or, in the case of youth officers or peer-led programmes, the marketing mediators, and also includes ticket schemes, extraneous activities associated with the main event, such as first-night parties, and the general atmosphere of the venue. 'Intrinsic' appeal refers to the nature of the cultural event or experience – the relevance to young people's own culture, of the art form, or version of the art form, in which the experience is presented, and the relevance of the content to their own interests and concerns.

Accordingly, venues which enhanced the extrinsic appeal of their premises and programme were those seeking to remove the physical barriers to attendance, while venues and organisations whose marketing energy re-orientated the art form itself, in order to reveal its potential to appeal to young people, were those attempting to dispel psychological barriers. Many venues and organisations were engaged in a continuing process of experimentation, devising programmes and evolving strategies which took both physical and psychological barriers into account. However, while some of the larger and well-established venues and organisations employed a full marketing department to publicise their programmes for young people as appropriately and effectively as possible, representatives from others observed that they used most of their funding to enhance the cultural experience itself, and consequently there was little left for sophisticated marketing techniques. The education manager of one orchestra, who claimed concerts were regularly over-subscribed, said they spent their funding 'on projects rather than on publicity', and the curator of a small regional art gallery made the same point. Another respondent contended that although their programme for primary schools had been very well received, they would need 'targeted funding' in order to promote a similar range of activities in secondary schools.

3.5.1 The extrinsic appeal of a cultural event or experience

i. The appeal of material incentives (overcoming physical barriers)

Ticket schemes and discounts
In considering the following initiatives, it is worth bearing in mind that, unless the availability of various concessions is intended to be more than 'a one-off gimmick' (see previous chapter), and is integrated into a long-term commitment to sustaining a younger audience, experience suggests that it will almost certainly have a limited effect on audience attendance.

The majority of orchestras run ticket schemes whereby a certain number of tickets for concerts aimed at a younger audience are free or available at a discount. One orchestra claimed that the young people taking advantage of free tickets tended to be those studying music for GCSE and A level. However, an orchestra elsewhere affirmed the success of its community programme in encouraging people of all ages to attend their series of subsidised family concerts.

Some theatres claimed the success of the Test Drive the Arts Scheme. One provincial theatre provided 20 free seats for youth group members at each production in the 'main house'.

Reflecting the trend in small-scale venues, the director of a prominent metropolitan theatre recently announced an action plan to attract younger audiences. In order to encourage young people to performances of a new play about bullying, tickets were to be reduced, after the first month, from £29 to £5 for first-time theatre-goers. For the further benefit of younger audiences, it was also intended to stage free plays on concrete walkways outside the theatre.

A new art gallery, widely acclaimed by the national media for its successful union of 'access and excellence', was due to open in the autumn of 1999. Publicity material drew attention to the fact that suggestions from local residents, including young people, were incorporated as far as possible into the design of the new building. Entrance to the gallery, its exhibitions and all other facilities, would be free.

The concessions and ticket schemes referred to above were seen to have achieved very positive results in terms of attendance. It may be worth noting that none of the venues concerned have relied on material incentives alone. They have produced a programme purported to be relevant to young people's concerns, and/or, they have made it a priority to offer them the opportunity of contributing their views on the appearance of the venue, the programme and the presentation of the art form itself.

In some venues, various free social events are held to coincide with performance nights as an incentive to attendance. One regional theatre uses lighting and special effects to create a club atmosphere, and organises first-night parties with free drinks available for young people attending the performance. At a young people's arts venue elsewhere, 'club nights' are held every Friday and Saturday as purely social events. They are generally regarded as 'a good night out', but allegedly they also succeed in encouraging young people to return, to attend and, or, participate in, the wide variety of arts events arranged with local and touring professional artists.

Free transport

Providing free tickets may act as an incentive to attendance, particularly if concessions are built in to a long-term plan. However, it is frequently pointed out that ticket concessions for an arts event are only a partial solution to any perceived physical barrier. In order for many young people to attend a cultural venue, they need help with transport costs, or, particularly in isolated rural areas, the provision of transport itself. So far, only a few venues have been able to address this problem for the benefit of young attenders. For example, one peer-led art gallery project now provides travelling expenses for young workshop leaders and for young volunteers involved in mounting exhibitions. By contrast, a flourishing school-gallery collaboration elsewhere attributed its inability to attract young people from more remote communities to the limited availability of school and public transport.

Mobile arts facilities in some areas are helping to resolve this problem. In a sparsely populated area in the north, a mobile multi-media studio tours isolated villages, liaising with youth workers and involving young people in planning the kind of provision they need. In the suburbs outside London, mobile facilities from a young people's arts venue visit local housing estates to alert young residents to the cultural experiences available to them.

ii. The appeal of the marketing medium (overcoming psychological barriers)

Using a communication system which is appealing and familiar to young people

Many organisations acknowledged the importance of creating access for young people through their own preferred medium, and valued the Internet for its 'street credibility'. A number of them had their own websites, and many others were in the process of setting one up, often involving young people in the design and technical aspects of the task.

At one art gallery a new project for the current year involves eight young people in creating a website with a multi-media producer. The priority is to promote world-wide participation in debate among young people about contemporary art. Elsewhere, the website for a major symphony orchestra includes audio and video extracts from concerts which young people have attended and participated in.

Although a great many young people do not have access to the Internet at home, it is becoming increasingly available in schools, in libraries and 'on the street'. The arts organisations referred to here have recognised that the Web is definitely 'cool', and affirm that it is a valuable marketing tool, especially when young people are involved in designing and running a website themselves.

Marketing through mediators with street credibility

It was widely believed that young people who have little experience of the arts are more likely to be persuaded to attend cultural events by people they feel they can trust, who accept the 'physical' and 'psychological' barriers they may perceive, and appreciate their preferences. This role was frequently seen best performed by their peers, or by members of the youth service.

The value of 'peer-led' activities is illustrated by the perceived success of two initiatives mentioned earlier: first, the recent art gallery project where an advisory group of young people chose and developed programmes for their peers to accompany exhibitions; and secondly, the deployment of the Test Drive the Arts scheme in Bradford, whereby ten young Asians were recruited through focus groups to act as arts ambassadors for local theatres within their own community.

Many organisations across all art forms valued their association with the youth service as a highly effective means of reaching young people out of school, especially those who had no access to cultural experiences at home. A 'very well-supported' youth theatre in the South Midlands is funded jointly by the education and youth services, and at least two major orchestras regularly send musicians to work in youth clubs, often working on a fusion of classical and non-classical styles. The repeated portrayal in the data of youth workers as individuals with credibility among young people would seem to underline their considerable potential as advocates of the arts.

Marketing the event in terms of young people's own culture

An arts worker at a purpose-built youth arts venue drew attention to the importance of a 'non-judgemental' approach to youth culture in encouraging young people to experiment with art forms that were unfamiliar to them. Such an approach recalls the two-way culture proposed earlier. Many arts co-ordinators agreed that traditional forms of 'high art' may be perceived as in some way elitist, or constrained within a set of rigid conventions. Young people may feel they are expected to conform to expected patterns of behaviour, or unwritten rules, at traditional theatres, galleries and concert halls. They may also have unfavourable preconceptions of an art form itself, fearing perhaps that it may be unintelligible, as well as unenjoyable.

The typology of successful strategies continues, following the extrinsic-intrinsic continuum referred to above. Accordingly, young people's experience of publicity material, and how it is presented to them, will be considered next. The analysis then moves on, to the nature of the venue, its ambience, and the social and cultural opportunities available to a younger audience.

Linguistic credibility: through publicity

In order to compete with young people's habitual interests and leisure activities, many organisations and venues deliberately adopt the prevalent idioms of youth culture to market events and activities for this age group. Given the powerful drive in many adolescents to preserve their loyalty to current peer norms, it seems to be widely recognised (in recent health education campaigns, for example), that informal and colloquial linguistic styles enhance the image of any organisation seeking to appeal to young people as a whole. Examples here include the use of the term 'art clubbing' to promote a school–gallery collaboration in Gallery Week. A major orchestral concert, the culmination of a series of small-scale events, was advertised as 'The Big Gig'; and for the duration of the project, the orchestra concerned promoted its integral website on brightly coloured postcards, exhorting its potential audience to 'link to other cool music and club sites'.

Linguistic credibility: in presenting/interpreting the event

It has been argued that for young people to become discerning arts consumers, they need to assimilate a 'critical vocabulary' (ACGB, 1992:5). After detailed consultation with young people, one art gallery recorded the view that the traditional labelling style of exhibits was 'off-putting', and inaccessible because of the formality and complexity of the language. Another gallery addressed the problem of linguistic access through a recent 'Curating Project' in which seven young people were invited to write alternative labels for a selection of the works on display. Participants were encouraged to use their own responses from initial discussions in pairs, and then to create their own labels to communicate an individual interpretation. The resulting labels were displayed to complement the existing, traditional ones, and the gallery recorded the value of the project in 'highlighting the potential of this alternative voice'.

It might at least be possible that the willingness of the young people here to engage with works of art sprang from the freedom to use their own language to shape their initial responses, and from the self-esteem acquired from having the validity of their responses accepted alongside more formally expressed interpretations. Could such a 'non-judgemental' strategy kindle a latent interest in the arts among other groups of young people, giving them confidence in their ability both to interpret and to express that interpretation? From this position, it might be only a small step towards gradually introducing them to the more formal or sophisticated language used in interpretation in various cultural contexts. In order to avoid any sense of imposition from their point of view, the continuing validity of their own language would need to be clearly recognised in a 'two-way' osmosis, in which each of the cultural vocabularies would be open to assimilation of elements from the other.

Transforming the experience of a traditional mainstream venue (with its particular conventions/language/etiquette)

A number of traditional cultural centres have endeavoured to appeal to younger audiences by installing facilities reflecting their habitual leisure interests so that the venue acquires the ambience and ethos of venues familiar, acceptable and accessible to young people.

Significantly, young people who contributed ideas for updating a northern art gallery offered a holistic perspective, rather than views on what occurred exclusively in the exhibition spaces. The exterior of the building, the look of publicity material, the atmosphere of the foyer and the café all appeared to affect its credibility. Their sensitivity to the ambience of the gallery environment, and the welcome it implied, highlights a comprehensive interpretation of access which cultural venues may need to embrace if they wish to encourage young people to be regular visitors.

Creating new venues specifically designed for youth arts

An alternative strategy for creating an ambience where young people feel at ease is to build arts venues specifically designed for them. A 'multi-arts' venue in East Anglia, purpose-built for young people ten years ago, presents arts events alongside 'club nights' to attract a wider audience. Elsewhere, a new 'multi-arts' venue, supported by the Arts Council Lottery Fund, includes a multi-media floor (for graphics, DTP, design, photography, and computer-based arts), a broadcasting standard TV studio, and studios for dance and sound recording. Phase One, the creation of a performance venue, café and restaurant, is virtually complete, and several stand-up comedians have already performed there. It is worth noting that both arts and social facilities were regarded as integral to the total cultural experience.

Transferring the event to an alternative venue oriented to 'youth culture'

To some extent schools can be regarded as youth venues in that most young people are very familiar with them. However, schools have to accommodate the priorities of many different groups of adults. Consequently, even when they do attempt to integrate elements of youth culture, administrative and curricular structures may, perhaps inevitably, have a modifying effect on young people's original ideas. Furthermore, theatre-in-education, for example, can be subject to a 'multiplicity of aims' (Harland et al., 1998); in some cases, the artistic experience may become subservient to the message it attempts to convey, either in its intrinsic quality or in the way it is related to particular areas of the curriculum.

Nevertheless, professional artists from many performing arts organisations liaise with teachers to perform in schools. Some art galleries and museums operate loan schemes for schools, while others hold exhibitions in institutions where exhibition space is available.

With regard to young people's own 'out-of-school' venues, a well-established art gallery in the south-west recently included a club-based installation/intervention in a gallery-based exhibition, while five clubs in other major cities hosted a multi-media installation on tour.

Radio can be an alternative venue for young people, especially for the socially or geographically isolated, and also perhaps for the disabled. One art gallery recently collaborated with a local radio network on a debate specifically aimed at younger listeners. Hosted by young volunteers, the debate was recorded live in front of an audience of around 45 young people and ten gallery staff.

The flexibility and informality of mobile arts facilities

As explained earlier, two powerful 'psychological' barriers to young people's attendance were the perceived formality of traditional arts venues and the unfamiliarity of the art forms themselves. Like any inhabitants of isolated communities, young people in rural areas, and those on socially and geographically peripheral city housing estates, can be very insular in their perceptions of the outside world. They may be even more diffident than their peers elsewhere in relation to unfamiliar experience. For these young people, alternative arts provision in the form of mobile facilities was in several cases believed to be the most appropriate introduction to a wider culture.

According to research referenced earlier, (Mass Observation, 1990 and Harris Research Centre, 1993a), paucity of information pertaining to arts events was frequently alleged to be the reason for non-attendance. Many organisations contacted for this study recommended the strategy of publicising events for young people 'on the street' and through youth clubs, rather than constraining the thrust of promotion through more formal channels.

Moreover, some young people appear to find the formality and expected patterns of behaviour and interpretation prevailing in traditional cultural centres uniformly unpalatable. The alleged popularity of initiatives in alternative venues may suggest that if young people are given an opportunity to encounter 'high culture' informally, on their own familiar territory, they may feel less 'turned off' or threatened by what they would regard in traditional venues as a potentially irrelevant or demoralising experience. Thus it was proposed that if they feel free to respond to an art form on their own terms, they may come to reappraise their preconceptions about its irrelevance and unintelligibility. Arguably, such a shift in perspective may stir their enthusiasm to investigate art forms in a less familiar, more challenging environment

3.5.2 The intrinsic appeal of a cultural event or experience

i. Relevance of the art form to young people's own culture (overcoming psychological barriers)

The 'cultural hybrid'
This appears to be a contemporary phenomenon which might be defined as the integration of elements of popular culture with those of a 'highbrow', traditional cultural form or event in order to make the latter more accessible. Recent well-known examples might include *Shakespeare in Love*. This film exploited the 'true life-story' appeal of an interpretation of *Romeo and Juliet* as the dramatic expression of an episode in Shakespeare's life, and celebrated the sophistication of its audience with numerous allusions to the scenes and conventions of contemporary cinema within a historically 'accurate' Elizabethan setting. A trawl through the current publications of arts organisations yields various reflections of this genre.

Among recent adaptations of Shakespeare's plays aiming to attract younger audiences was a street musical performed at a major arts centre in the West Midlands. Based on *Macbeth*, and spirited from Scotland to Birmingham's club underworld, it was the third play in a series of youth-oriented musicals, commissioned by the arts centre's New Work Trust, which combine the talents of young people, recruited through schools and youth groups, with those of professional artists.

A musical organisation with a deliberately eclectic approach offers young people opportunities in as many different genres as possible. Programmes which may include a baroque chamber orchestra alongside African drummers and two rock bands, appeal to young people in the first instance through their sheer novelty, but the excitement of this initial experience is claimed to generate an enthusiasm which can be successfully sustained.

Reflecting a current interest in 'melding' the contrasting styles of classical and non-classical dance, one youth arts venue recently organised several major 'crossover' events. Well-established contemporary dance companies came and gave performances alongside young people, in an exchange of professional and vernacular club styles.

A pertinent example from the visual arts might be the major regional exhibition that aimed to challenge artistic convention by creating 'unexpected relationships between areas of culture normally considered apart'. The dynamic for the exhibition derived from the creation of a ready-made exhibition template from cultural references in the lyrics of a critically acclaimed contemporary band. Their allusions to a wide range of twentieth century artists has, according to gallery publicity, 'led to an unexpected audience for avant-garde ideas – teenagers from a variety of backgrounds and levels of education that might not otherwise have heard of abstract expressionism, let alone postmodernism or conceptual art'. The band are 'passionate advocates' of their particular regional culture and identity; thus their work combines 'the international avant-garde and … regionalism'.

In levelling culture, this exhibition also anticipated levelling audiences, since teenagers' and non-specialists' expertise in interpretation would equal that of habitual gallery visitors. Accordingly, it was intended to contribute to current debate on the 'display and demarcation of culture', especially between museums and academic communities. Evidence of the audit may indicate that the 'demarcation', or division, between traditional and youth culture might need to be dispelled by such departures from traditional forms of presentation, if an accessible and credible two-way culture is to flourish.

Tailoring an event to accommodate young people's spectating habits

Most young people are used to operating computers and seeking entertainment from television, video and the cinema. They expect, and are used to responding to, frequent interruptions, such as advertisements, rapid scene changes and alternative camera shots. Accordingly, they may well expect to be able to initiate changes of stimuli for themselves when less familiar cultural experiences fail to engage their attention. Possible strategies for meeting these expectations might include:

- interactive features to sustain concentration;
- using cinematic techniques, such as alternative perspectives of a single event or experience, which offer a range of stylistically different interpretations of a single idea (in music, for example, a variety of styles on a variety of instruments).

Bearing these considerations in mind, it may be that multi-media events are particularly well-suited to the spectating patterns of contemporary young people. Significantly, a conspicuous number of initiatives recorded in the data offered young people access to a multi-media experience.

In the performing arts, musicals *per se* involve music, dance, theatre and visual effects; the plethora of musicals currently produced with young audiences in mind attests to the popularity of this genre. A southern arts marketing agency is encouraging all the theatres within its remit to incorporate a 'multi-layered experience' within their foyers to generate an atmosphere similar to that encountered by young people in clubs. The purpose-built youth venues referred to earlier all offer multi-media opportunities, through the provision of facilities in a range of media and, or, as single experiences involving various media simultaneously.

A range of media was seen as particularly appealing to young people at risk of social exclusion. One venue is currently working on a six month multi-media initiative, 'Motion', involving visual artists, a writer and dancers to create a performance piece which will go on tour to 'unstructured' venues, such as local housing estates and youth clubs.

According to respondents, persuading young people to engage in 'high' culture means convincing them of its relevance to them, both as individuals and as members of their peer group. Challenging young people's preconceptions of traditional art forms and expected modes of interpretation, by endorsing a 'two-way culture', and by giving them the freedom to respond in a way which is both accessible and acceptable to them, could be the means of eliciting the sustained commitment which all 'arts ambassadors' aim to instil.

ii. Relevance of the content to young people's interests and concerns (overcoming psychological barriers)

'Real-life' relevance

Ensuring the relevance of the art form is believed to be one of the most effective marketing strategies Many organisations enhance the standing of their activities for 14–18 year olds by ensuring they perceive the content addressed by the art form as relevant to their everyday lives. This strategy offers a wide range of opportunities to the theatre in particular.

In a move that reflects a recognisable trend among many grassroots venues, a major national theatre has staged a new play aimed at younger audiences concerned with bullying in the playground. Moreover, in order to sustain the momentum of this initiative, the theatre has secured sponsorship from a national business organisation to encourage well-known international playwrights to contribute plays, on themes relevant to young people, for performance in its auditoria.

Elsewhere, an apparently thriving youth theatre specialises in bringing together professional artists and 14–25 year olds. In addition to performances by touring professional companies, the 1999 summer season included a 'young bands music platform' (for under 18s), and *The Child Inside*, a new play written with the help of local teenage mothers and scripted by a local playwright, which would be touring schools and youth centres.

Humorous perspectives

The co-ordinator of a schools and gallery initiative in a largely rural author-
ity commented on the effectiveness of demonstrating an appreciation of
young people's own culture in choosing 'relevant' exhibitions. One of the
most popular recent events, a display of sculpture on contemporary themes,
had offered a humorous perspective – it included a pair of Doc Martens
made of metal cans – which dispelled any anxieties about formality, and the
prevalence of bright colours and a relaxed atmosphere engendered a very
positive response from younger visitors.

The education officer of an art gallery in the Midlands referred to a bid
submitted to the DfEE for a project exploring the entitlement of young
people to 'a good-quality cultural experience'. According to the data, the
dynamic for such an experience might derive from a sensitive response to
young people's own endorsement of the 'two-way' culture discernible in
many differentiated versions here.

3.6 ATTENDANCE AND PARTICIPATION

Virtually all initiatives recorded in the audit include an element of participation. Depending on the definition of the terms 'audience attendance' and
'participation', it could be argued that, if audience attendance itself is to
be a positive experience, it will involve the audience in 'participating' as
critical listeners and/or spectators, as interpreters and, crucially, with respect
to young people here, as representatives of their peers.

It would, therefore, be possible to represent attendance by young
people in the following categories:

i.   participation as 'critical spectator' (interpretation)
ii. participation as 'impresario' (advisory, marketing, hosting event)
iii. participation as 'artist' (producing, performing, creating,
     composing)

Both kinds of dance initiative referred to in this chapter (for boys and for the
disabled), emphasise participation, but in each case attendance is implicit in
the informal audience role which habitually occurs when participants act as
spectators and interpreters of one another's work. The activity may develop
their listening, spectating, and interpreting skills in an informal setting with
their peers, and, it could be argued, serves as an introduction to, and preparation for, the more sustained version of such skills required for the experience of audience attendance *per se* (type i). It seems that many arts organisations would contend that participation as either impresario or artist (types
ii and iii) has proved to be a very effective means of audience development.

3.6.1 Audience attendance *per se*: participation as critical spectator

Representatives from all art forms advocated some form of advance preparation in order for attendance at a venue to be a positive experience. Pre-performance 'workshops' or discussions were frequently seen as prerequisite for engaging young people as active (receptive and reflective) members of the audience at any cultural experience. However, as acknowledged above, the emphasis tended to be on participation as impresario and artist rather than as critical spectator, particularly in relation to music and the performing arts.

Few initiatives in the audit sought to attract a young audience without initially engaging their interest through participation in some kind of related activity. Moreover, the majority of organisations that offer free tickets, and other material incentives, appear to recognise that these alone will not cause the shift in perception required to sustain any long-term commitment. It may be worth noting that of the five specific initiatives here which aimed to attract young people as critical spectators, rather than as direct participants, four were from the visual arts.

At a northern gallery, for example, staff were working with 16–18 year olds on a project funded by the ACE and Crayola, to explore art, design and architecture. This gallery's approach was perceived to be distinctive in that it was 'a more introspective model', less 'hands-on' and primarily concerned with interpretation.

A gallery of contemporary art recently completed a project with 14–18 year olds recruited through youth clubs, in which exhibitions were used as a starting point for them to work out their own interpretations through reflecting on their personal preferences. Elsewhere, focus groups had illuminated young people's views on approaches to interpretation. Significantly in relation to other evidence in the audit, the gallery concerned reported, firstly, that participants felt confident in their ability to form their own opinions and, secondly, that they wanted more interactive interpretation, alongside a more interactive experience within the gallery as a whole.

With regard to the performing arts, a theatre which drew a steady audience of young people from local youth groups offered them an opportunity to 'become acquainted with the internal workings of the professional theatre' (ACGB, 1992:25), in addition to discussions introducing specific productions. Pertinently, they were also given a chance to express their reactions to the performance to members of theatre staff, who subsequently visited the youth clubs to glean responses.

The commitment to listening to their reactions may be particularly important in convincing young people of the value of their role as members of the audience; they may need to be persuaded that the audience is 'an essential part of the experience', the other half of the equation, rather than merely a commercial necessity.

3.6.2 Participation as artist or as impresario

The second type of participation involved young people in an *impresario/adviser* role: representing audience needs in 'peer-led' initiatives in an advisory capacity (e.g. on the nature of the programme and, or, the marketing strategy) or as impresarios (e.g. with responsibility for marketing, for hosting the event and for all the associated administration). The third type of participation involved young people in an *artist* role: producing/performing/participating in workshops.

Examples of both kinds of participation have recurred throughout the main typology of marketing strategies. Some arts organisations have had significant success in attracting new attenders through involving young people in planning programmes, marketing, organising and hosting events, and in mediator roles, running peer-led workshops and performances. For one gallery, 'responding to young people's informed advice' over an extended period of time has allowed staff to 'fine-tune' its services, and has resulted in a clear commitment to 'the value of peer-led work in planning and delivering an innovative and apparently unique programme'.

Opportunities to participate as 'artist' prevailed across all art forms. Moreover, although participation was widely believed to be one of the most effective methods of audience development, many organisations recognised the value of participation *per se*, and were committed to engaging young people 'in the disciplines and pleasures of learning and performing'. For many of those concerned with the socially excluded, participation was explicitly an end in itself.

3.7 EMERGING ISSUES

3.7.1 Perceptions of effective strategies

According to the respondents consulted in this review, the most successful strategies for breaking down 'psychological' barriers were:

i.   developing close and sustained consultation with young people;
ii. building and maintaining good working relationships with members of the Youth Service.

According to many organisations here, youth workers were highly 'significant others', who meet young people 'on their own ground' and were trusted by them to represent their concerns. Where informal networks of communication were already in existence, small-scale 'organic' growth was frequently perceived to be an effective strategy.

iii. recognition of the need for relevance, of the 'marketing', the 'medium' and the 'content' of the product, to generate engagement, to dispel erroneous preconceptions of both arts venues and art forms, and to give young people the freedom to respond in a way which is accept able and accessible to them. Such concern for relevance may reaffirm the potential of a 'two-way' culture.

If such a culture were to be nurtured, possible strategies might include:

- innovative and imaginative programming, reflecting the spectating patterns of young people's own culture, for example in terms of multi-media events and the evolution of 'cultural hybrids';
- unconventional, youth-oriented marketing techniques, which exploit the systems of communication young people themselves prefer, and acknowledge the validity of their own cultures, both for the promotion of an artistic event and for its interpretation.

iv. a commitment to the importance of sustaining momentum: according to the evidence here, young people's regular attendance will not be secured by enticing them with short-term, purely material incentives. It was widely believed that a long-term impact was much more likely to occur if young people were allowed to 'colonise' a venue or an art form. Many respondents insisted on the importance of allowing a generous amount of time for initiatives to develop 'organically'. Young people need time:

- to overcome any peer-influenced preconceptions or personal diffidence;
- to contribute their own ideas to a momentum at once dynamic and sustainable; and
- to realise those ideas in a way which makes the venue or art form more appealing to themselves and their peers.

In practical terms, the respondents considered that this requires:

- long-term funding and recognition of the need for preparation, in order for young people to make sense, as critical spectators, of what they see;
- preparation for the nature of the venue and, or art form, as well as for the particular performance or exhibition.

v. acknowledgement of the particular value of a holistic approach for young people unfamiliar with arts events and venues (particularly those perceived to be at risk of social exclusion); presentation of the cultural experience accordingly in:

- a 'geographically' and, or 'socially', more accessible context (local communities in estates, clubs and youth groups);
- a 'conceptually' more accessible context (everyday concerns such as employment, economic regeneration, young people's rights, sport, and health issues).

It has been almost impossible to identify any initiatives that aim to encourage young people to attend an arts event without also engaging in some form of participation either beforehand or during the event itself. Even where the emphasis of the marketing strategy is on the extrinsic appeal of free tickets and discounts, the material attraction is frequently supported by focused discussions, in order for young people to find a way in, socially and conceptually, to both the venue and the medium, as well as to the immediate issues of the play and the specific interpretation of the performance.

As the foregoing review has underlined, participation in its broadest sense would seem to be treated as a prerequisite for audience attendance by the majority of young people at cultural venues. It was widely believed as unrealistic to expect them to spend time, and possibly money, voluntarily to attend an unfamiliar event, in a totally unfamiliar context, as passive listeners or spectators. Arts organisations agreed that for young people with no previous experience of the cultural dimension under scrutiny, such events may seem irrelevant to their own lives, unrelated to their own experience and associated with social groups perceived by them to be very different from, and possibly unsympathetic to, themselves.

According to many of the cultural venues consulted in the audit, the dynamic for 'a good-quality cultural experience' might evolve from a sensitive response to young people's own endorsement of a 'two-way' culture. From this perspective, a culture that openly embraces the culture of young people becomes peculiarly dynamic; it is subject to the faster pace of change, the accelerated transience of youth culture itself. Accordingly, a commitment to the innumerable possibilities of a two-way culture would demand uncompromising flexibility, in order to sustain continuous refinement and redefinition.

Some traditional cultural institutions might need to change their perceptions of young people as potential spectators: they might still regard young people as receptive material, ready to be instilled with an uncritical appreciation of their existing programmes. They might have to accept that young people already operate as a potential audience independently, with their own tastes, their own culture, their own preferences and powers of discrimination, and that these need to be acknowledged and addressed by any arts organisations intending to cultivate their attendance.

3.7.2 Differences between art forms and the nature of young people's audience engagement

There was some indication that the task of encouraging attendance in art galleries may be perceived as slightly different from that in the performing arts. The co-ordinator of one gallery speculated that the nature of the experience of engagement might be more introspective compared to that in music and the theatre. Therefore it may be more of a challenge to engage and sustain young people's attention, particularly that of 14–18 year olds. According to some respondents, young people's concentration span may be shorter than that of adults for two reasons: firstly they are physically more active; secondly, with regard to the sophisticated spectating patterns of contemporary youth culture, they may expect frequent changes of stimulation.

Several art gallery representatives seemed to imply that the visual arts may be intrinsically more difficult for young people to interpret, because music and the performing arts communicate feelings as well as ideas in a more immediate way, and thus invite a more immediate, active response. Whereas the appeal of the visual arts, until comparatively recently, has been static and thus, literally, reflective, and therefore possibly more conducive to an introspective interpretation. On the other hand, young people may find it hard to see any value in the audience role in the performing arts and music, because they have to watch other people doing something, and may perceive members of the audience to have an inferior role to that of the performer.

In the visual arts (apart from pavement artists and the increasingly popular craft workshops) it is much less usual to watch visual artists at work; people in art galleries and museums tend to be in the role of spectator. Consequently, although initially it may be more difficult to engage young people in the intellectual challenge of interpretation, they may be more willing to participate in purely interpretative activities in the visual arts than in music and the performing arts, because they can see that they are 'performing' the same role as everyone else, and it may, therefore, be easier to convince them that the role of interpreter *per se*, is of value. Perhaps this might explain why the initiatives emphasising participation as critical spectator (type i) tended to occur in the visual arts.

3.7.3 Whose responsibility?

One education officer observed that the subject of our research concerned marketing rather than education and was thus outside his brief – a telling indication, perhaps, of how some arts organisations may see their relationship with young people.

In one theatre, until recently, marketing young people's activities had been the responsibility of the education department. Since being taken over by the marketing department, it was apparent that 'the profile of the work has risen – both externally and, importantly, internally'. Now that the expertise and the resources of the marketing department control young people's activities, its status was perceived to have risen not only in the local community but also within the theatre itself. Commitment to working with young people throughout all departments of an arts organisation may be a significant factor if they are to benefit from the opportunities provided for them.

3.7.4 Risks to traditional audiences

Many mainstream venues acknowledged the risk of balancing 'the variety of the work so that you don't detach the audience which has supported you over many years, while you also encourage a younger audience'. Some theatres and orchestras successfully attract audiences of all ages by ensuring that programmes include material 'relevant' to young people in addition to the standard repertoire. Other strategies include marketing both the venue and the programme through a medium with street credibility. For some cultural institutions, however, the need to reconcile the expectations of their traditional audiences with those of informal contemporary culture remained an urgent responsibility.

3.7.5 Evaluation

In spite of vigorous affirmations of success from co-ordinators of the initiatives described here, the positive effects of their marketing and programming strategies were not necessarily substantiated by systematic evaluation.

In the case of some longer-term projects, a series of annual or 'interim' reports contributed to a continuing system of regular review. One gallery's third annual report on the progress of a young people's advisory group attributed the success of its young people's programme to the crucial role of 'consultation over an extended period of time'. Education Extra is a national organisation which aims to put after-school activities within the reach of every child. A report on one Education Extra project at a multi-arts centre in an inner-city area noted that young people who said that they had taken part in art or drama activities out of school, achieved significantly higher GCSE results than those who said they did not (though the analysis was unable to shed any light on the direction of causality in the observed association). By contrast, an interim report on a project involving young people in promoting live arts events recorded difficulties encountered, including timing (which had depended to a considerable extent on funding), and re-organisation in the youth service.

A lack of evaluations capable of studying behavioural changes in young people is also evident in the museums sector. Although various case studies of projects in museums and galleries with young people have been published (Selwood et al., 1995; Rider and Illingworth, 1997), to date, no evidence is currently available as to whether particular types of activity have actually contributed to changing institutions' visitor profiles.

A number of organisations pointed out that funding was spent on improving opportunities for young people, without conducting any systematic evaluation. However, the majority averred that evaluation was vital, and formed an integral component of all activities. An orchestra's education officer insisted that participants completed evaluation forms after all projects; staff from one provincial theatre meet young audience members at their own youth centres after performances, to see whether the experience has stimulated them to attend future productions. The main evaluation for a multi-media initiative in a contemporary art gallery took the form of a video made by young participants who had particularly appreciated the tactile and interactive approach to interpretation. The video itself was inaccessible at the time of writing, but the accompanying report noted the value of the project for first time gallery visitors, as an opportunity to express their preferences.

Given the unavailability of systematic evaluations for many initiatives at the time of the audit (e.g. the evaluation of the New Audiences Programme was not yet available), informally reported evidence of any long-term impact on extending young people's attendance must be regarded, at best, as inconclusive. The observations of those involved on long-term projects, on the advantages of their extended duration, may, however, lend credence to the view that any rigorous evaluation might best fulfil its purpose by implementing a longitudinal approach, in order to examine whether or not the initiatives under scrutiny achieve any impact on young people's patterns of cultural behaviour.

3.7.6 Respecting the uninterested

This study springs from the belief that the arts and cultural venues are of potential benefit to the well-being of everyone, individually and collectively. However, we risk working on an erroneous assumption if we insist that everyone is bound to find some area of the arts appealing *per se*, and that it is just a matter of exposing people to every possible arts experience in order for them to find their niche.

The potential value of participation in the arts for socially excluded young people was repeatedly endorsed by respondents working with 'the disaffected' and many arts enthusiasts would argue with passion for the superior value of the arts over other 'leisure' activities for all young people; competing for young people's attention (against sport, or the natural world, for example) becomes, for them, a pressing imperative.

Clearly, however, young people will decide for themselves and temptations to generalise about young people must be resisted. Fowle's (1997) observation may be salient here; he warned that it may be patronising to those who 'simply see themselves as people and believe that their opinions and awareness of larger issues are as relevant as any adult', to lump them together into a single category of 'young people'. Young people are individuals; and between the ages of 14 and 18 loyalty to prevailing peer culture may be in painful and recurring conflict with the adolescent quest for self-identity. Personal considerations – life experience, aspirations, aptitude, interests and so on – will make the interpretations and responses of each one of them unique. Hence, there may be many young people for whom fulfilment comes in some other way; they may not feel the need to relate to the arts at all. This needs to be fully acknowledged in any attempt to extend their cultural experience.

'I AM NEW': YOUNG PEOPLE'S ACCOUNTS OF ACCESSING CULTURAL VENUES

Karen Halsey and Kay Kinder

4.1 BACKGROUND

4.1.1 Introduction

This chapter reports on the component of the project which sought to collect the views of 20 young people, aged 14–18, in order to investigate their experiences of attendance; and to tease out key factors which accounted for different levels of attendance among the sample. The research focused on four key areas:

- general attitudes towards arts/cultural organisations;
- levels and experience of attendance;
- key factors which prevent or promote attendance; and
- recommendations made by young people for improving attendance.

4.1.2 The sample

Given that the research focus was to be on the attitudes of young people and the language they used, the sample size was not meant in any way to convey representative findings. Nevertheless, in selecting the 20 young people, a main concern was to incorporate a range of variables, in terms of age, gender, ethnicity, location, daytime activity and involvement in the arts. The sample's characteristics were:

- Eight of the young people were aged 14–15 years and the remaining twelve aged 16–18 years.
- Five geographical locations (Leeds, London, Mansfield, North Yorkshire and Buckinghamshire) were targeted: 13 of the young people lived in urban areas and seven in rural areas.
- Eleven of the sample were in school (eight at KS4 and three in the sixth form), five were at FE college, two in vocational training and two in employment.
- The sample included 3 young people from Asian and African-Caribbean backgrounds.

The sample was divided into those with high, medium and low attendance, producing three distinct groups of respectively five, six and nine young people. Low attendance was characterised as young people with few or no accounts of attending arts or cultural events, medium attenders tended to recollect some such experiences that had occurred largely through the mediation of school or family, while high attenders were those who described attendance as a voluntary and frequent leisure-time activity, either focusing particularly on one art form or engaging in different arts experiences. Not surprisingly, those who were very involved in the arts (e.g. studying the arts or participating regularly), were typically those who also reported high levels of attendance, while those with no arts interests fell into the category of low-level attendance.

4.1.3 Interviewing the sample

Interviews typically ran for 40–50 minutes. In that time, the young people were invited to comment on five different categories of cultural activity:

Art　　art galleries and exhibitions
Dance　ballet, tap, African and modern
Drama　theatre performances, musicals, comedies
Heritage castles, historic houses and museums
Music　classical concerts, choral performances, jazz bands and piano recitals

It should be noted that the final category deliberately omitted reference to popular music as access to this kind of music is unlikely to need encouragement.

　　During both the interviews and subsequent analysis, it was apparent that this sample of young people largely confirmed existing research about what prevents their access to arts and cultural events. Rather than presenting startling new findings, this part of the report attempts to illustrate the way young people construct their images and experiences of arts and cultural attendance, and pays particular attention to the language they used. Finally, by way of introduction, it is noteworthy that not one of the 20 young people recollected encountering any of the type of youth-oriented initiatives outlined in the previous chapter.

4.2 YOUNG PEOPLE'S ATTITUDES TOWARDS CULTURAL VENUES

4.2.1 The importance of the arts and culture

When asked, 'Personally, how important are the arts, and [cultural] venues to you?', six out of the 20 young people felt they were *not important* with the riders that they had other things to do; or arts were only important if being considered as a career option:

Not a lot, because there's other things that I would rather do (male, 15).

I am glad I have been to most of them and experienced them, but given the choice I wouldn't do them over something else … compared to being with your friends or going to watch the football or something like that, it hasn't got the same appeal (male, 17).

They are not the most important thing in my life to go and see, but I think other people should have their own opinion about them. I don't think they shouldn't be here. I think they should be here because there's like loads of people who like things like this, but it's just not me (female, 17).

The remaining 14 interviewees did see the arts as *important* to themselves, to varying degrees. The reasons arts had some currency for them included:

A *social opportunity*: Although the interviewees did not always suggest arts and cultural venues as places to spend an evening or a day out, one girl recognised the social aspects of these places: 'people can get together and have a good time' (female, 17).

Diversity and enrichment: Four interviewees felt that the arts represented diversity, something extra, which made life a bit more interesting. Without them, 'everybody would be scientists you know, it would be a very dull place' (male, 18).

Very [important] *I think they have a large part … especially the music has a large part in my personality itself. I enjoy them all, I enjoy going to places and seeing things and having variation. It's important* (female, 15).

The feel-good factor: Interviewees commented on the positive feelings they acquired as a consequence of attendance, while two spoke of the buzz of anticipation before going:

Every time I go and see something I am always on a bubbly high, just being involved in something cheers me up, my friends see a profound difference in me when I have been to see something (female, 15).

Promoting creativity: For one interviewee, arts and culture had mind-expanding qualities which he contrasted with the scientific world, where everything was 'black and white'. Hence, the arts were thought important for fostering creativity.

With science you have to have an answer, it's all formulas and stuff, whereas with this, it's just using your mind and seeing how far you can push your mind, what you can produce (male, 18).

A link with the past: Having established that arts and culture were sometimes thought to represent the 'old way of life', one 17 year old boy felt this was actually an important contribution, which should not be lost. Essentially, higher arts and culture connected today's society with the past:

They are extremely important in the way people are educated and it would be sad to see like... I can't imagine they would, but if, like, orchestras died and no one went. Because it's a big part of, like, history and where it came from and everything is important. So yes, it's all important today, as much as yesterday (male, 17).

A learning experience: Finally, arts and culture were perceived by four interviewees as important because they provided a learning experience:

I think they are important so that we learn about things and experience things and see what they are like, because you can't say 'I don't like it' unless you have been (female, 14).

I think it's important to know about all the different things. I think it's a good idea to because then you are just more knowledgeable on everything (female, 14).

It is worth emphasising that those who espoused the value of the arts, were those who also participated in them and attended most frequently.

Some of the young people spoke of an attitudinal swing in relation to their feelings towards the arts and culture. Of the twenty interviewees, there were six examples of increasing interest, and five incidences where enthusiasm was felt to have dwindled. Typically, increased positive attitudes were expressed as:

When I was at primary school I didn't really think much of art, and I quite like it now. I think as you get older your opinions do change (male, 18).

I am a lot more broad-minded about those things now, open to anything (male, 18).

I think [my attitude] has changed because I have become more interested in the deeper meaning of art and more interested in learning about history and things like that. At primary school it was all sort of, you had to concentrate on the fun of things of the museum instead of looking deeply into pictures, it was just a picture with paint on. So, I think it's changed in areas like you understand it, you have got a deeper understanding of everything to do with it and so it's more interesting nowadays (female, 14).

While attendance opportunities had increased the interest of some young people, for one individual enforced attendance led to disengagement and rejection. Speaking of attendance as an 'adult thing ... you were told to go and look', he felt as a young child, he could not appreciate the benefit of these things. Because adults were encouraging it, he was now 'going against it', an affirmation of his independence: 'I want to make my own decisions, sort of thing'.

Four young people remembered how as children they were more

'intrigued', keen to learn and 'more enthusiastic'. Growing up had some-how quelled this enthusiasm and as a consequence, the cultural venues were no longer as inviting:

> *I think I would have been more interested then on a general level, not get too deep into it. I think now the problem with me is, I have to have it, like, shoved in my face, 'Here it is, come and have a look', but maybe when I was younger, I would have been more jumped up and gone to all sort of things. So maybe I'm a little bit more laid back now about it* (female, 18).

> *I was probably quite interested in it when I was younger. I still am now, but I mean more when I was younger because I didn't know much about it, it was the intrigue. Now I know about it, I am still interested in it, it's useful to know, but not as much* (male, 16).

> *When you are younger you want to learn different things and get to know everything and try your best, but when you get older, you just think, 'Well I have done that, I can't be bothered any more', that's how I think anyway* (female, 17).

> *I used to love going to* [heritage places] *but I kind of grew out of it because it's not really interesting. It's just the same things, you keep on going there and it's all the same and it's just going on* (female, 15).

Lastly, one interviewee attributed her change in attitude to the time she left school. Her experience of arts and culture had always been linked with school and consequently she was purposefully putting arts and culture to one side,

> *I had left school, so I thought I have done enough of school, I have been there five or six years at high school, and I thought 'no, I had done my GCSE's, I need to get a job' and that* (female, 17).

4.2.2 Images of cultural venues

At the beginning of the interviews the young people were encouraged to verbalise their 'images' of the five categories of cultural venue by invitation to respond to such questions as 'what are art galleries like?, what are your feelings towards museums?, could you describe what a dance performance would be like?'. Given the levels of attendance evident among the sample, not surprisingly a number of the interviewees struggled with their answers. Nonetheless, their replies were revealing, especially as they represented an immediate, unrehearsed response towards such venues. The discourse of cultural anomie and self-exclusion surfaced in many of the answers, again closely matching previous research findings.

Art

These young people were often negative when asked to conjure up their images of art galleries. 'Quiet' and 'boring' were the most common perceptions, although this view was typically based on guesswork rather than real-life experience:

Quite boring, I have never been to one at all (female, 17).

I like art places, but it's a bit dull really and they are always quiet and I am not a person for quiet places. All paintings all over, older people walking around (female, 14).

One interviewee commented that the paintings were beautiful, but she still thought art galleries were boring and 'I don't like going'. Given that she clearly appreciated the artwork, it would seem to be the ambience, rather than the art form, *per se*, that she was uncomfortable with. Similarly, another noted:

Not that appealing, it's just in large rooms with large pictures in, and I appreciate the skill in doing them and individually appreciate the feeling of the painting, what they are trying to portray. But I don't like the crowded togetherness of lots of paintings on the wall and you walk past (male, 17).

One girl felt that TV presented an image of art-goers as being 'right snobby and they know what they are talking about'. Yet this same individual expressed a strong desire to visit her local art gallery, and it may be that anticipation of perceived 'snobbiness' (with its association of being excluded, feeling different and inferior) was a significant factor in preventing her attendance. Another individual, who had actually been to an art gallery, still described a typical attender as 'snooty, snobby ... there's nothing really for teenagers to look at and find interesting because it's either old art or really just odd looking art'.

Dance

The idea of watching ballet was not particularly appealing for several interviewees with typical comments including:

... not really my thing
it's not awful to watch, but I don't really find it that entertaining
I wouldn't really go, it's boring ...
I can't say it interests me.

Two interviewees stated they could not see the meaning behind ballet:

I don't like it, it's pointless (male, 15).
I just don't really see the story-line for the ballet (female, 17).

One respondent felt dance was largely a 'high-class, expensive' activity, while another commented on the formality of the occasion with 'people dressed up smart'. Those who could offer their images of dance described it as:

People in tights. People sometimes think of people in those big puffy skirts, but I like modern dance, modern ballet, so lots of dramatic things and music (female, 14).

Energetic, I watched on the TV that Lord of the Dance thing and that was quite good (female, 17).

People all dressed up smart, watching ballet and stuff like that (male, 18).

While actual attendance was low, there were a few examples of enthusiasm where young people were at least receptive to the idea of viewing a dance performance:

I would be really interested ... I really like all the line dancing and Irish dancing, I love it, so I haven't done it, but I would really enjoy a night watching that (female, 18).

Drama

The prevailing view of theatre attendance among the sample was that it was 'fun'. One 18 year old boy, currently taking an A level in theatre studies, described his anticipation. 'I really look forward to it, I get this sort of buzz before we even go. I think "yes, I am off to the theatre tonight!" and I can't wait to get there'. Another commented on the atmosphere and the feeling it created, which he felt was more powerful than watching a film at the cinema. Others appeared less intensely affected, but still saw theatre as a way of 'having a good time, having a laugh':

Sometimes it's really enjoyable, I wouldn't mind going to see a play at all, it's fun sometimes (male, 15).

I really like going to theatres and stuff, I like musicals and things like that. I think that's really good fun, I like that (female, 14).

Quite interesting, fun, they are often funny (female, 18).

One low attender imagined opera when asked to give his impressions of the theatre and consequently he thought of it as 'really, really boring'.

Heritage

Those who responded adversely to the idea of museums and historic venues, felt they were boring, sometimes intimidating and 'not for young people'. One 15 year old girl, who enjoyed dance and drama performances, saw historic places as 'eerie, scary places, just quite boring', with the explanation that 'history doesn't mean much to me'. Another interviewee commented 'it's good that you can get out, but it's just not for me'.

By contrast, those who appreciated such places, appeared to value their historic connections and the learning experience engendered within them. For some, this appreciation seemed to have developed from their schooling:

I think they are really interesting I suppose, because I have just done history A level, so things like cathedrals and castles and stately homes, you can see the heritage and the history of it and it's quite interesting (male, 18).

I have done history at GCSE and I have learnt more about it ... because I have learnt about the history ... to actually see history and also it's cool (male, 17).

It's interesting, and it has got history and I like history (female, 17).

That's interesting, because you find out what's old and a lot of history, different cultures (male, 15).

Music

Music events, like art, received the thumbs down from a number of the young people. When asked whether she would ever go to an evening of classical music, a 17 year old replied, quite emphatically, 'No, not at all because it's really baggy and sad'. This sentiment was echoed by others in the sample:

I wouldn't ever want to go, I just find it totally boring (female, 17).

I am not really interested at all, not that music. No, it's not for me (male, 16).

Only one girl out of the twenty interviewees, with high levels of participation, expressed positive views about the classical music tradition, 'I like [that] music a lot, I take a great interest in music and I am performing a lot of music'. Another suggested the fusion of classical music with modern ('electric violins') and for this reason thought that it would be 'pretty good'. Here, in effect, was an advocation of the cultural hybrid depicted in the previous chapter. The rest of the sample perceived classical music performances as formal occasions 'it's people that are dressed up in tuxedos with their opera glasses', often very long 'it's just sitting there for hours listening to some woman whining on' and not for young people 'I don't think classical music is aimed at our age group'.

4.2.3 Awareness of cultural venues: who are they for?

At the beginning of the interviews, an effort was made to assess the awareness of cultural venues among this 14–18 year old sample, by asking the question: 'In this area, what sort of places are there that you could go for a day or a night out?'.

Only heritage and the theatre received a mention, the former six times and the latter three times. Going to the cinema was the most frequent suggestion for a day or night out, with going to a pub, restaurant, bowling alley, the shops, a leisure centre, youth club and 'the ski dome' as next in order of preference. From these responses, it is possible to draw several conclusions. Arguably, the young people did not have art galleries, dance venues or concert halls within their immediate locale. Alternatively, they may have been available, but the young people were unaware of their existence. Or finally, they may have been aware of their presence but did not consider them as forms of leisure entertainment. Whatever the explanation, it would seem that arts and culture did not generally feature as automatic leisure choices among the young people in this sample. Significantly, preferred options included social opportunities and physical activity.

The interviewees were then asked 'who would and who would not' attend particular events. As with the question of their perceptions of galleries and theatre etc., in some cases, answers were based on experience, because the young person had actually been to a venue and could recall the audience make-up. Other interviewees, however, had no experience of attendance, so their responses were based on conjecture.

Of all the categories of cultural venue, drama proved to be the exception, in that drama was not perceived to exclude any particular age group and was therefore attended by 'everybody I think, a lot of people go to the theatre'. In contrast, other venues were seen as for enthusiasts, those who could actually understand the medium. As shown in the box below, references were regularly made to 'middle …' or 'upper class, rich and older' people.

Who goes to arts venues?

Visual Art

Enthusiasts: *Arty people … I think you have to be interested to go, so people who are interested in the artist and art generally* (female, 18).

Affluent: *My perception is that it's the rich. They like more classic stuff and not the more modern stuff* (male, 17).

Older people: *As I looked around when I went in there, it was definitely older people. There weren't many teenagers going round. There was actually a section which was Icons of Pop, so that attracted lots of teenagers and young people. In the big main bit with pictures of Jesus and stuff like that, you wouldn't get many in there* (male, 17).

Drama

Any age: *A wide range of people do. Children go to see like pantomimes and things, but there's like older people and young people, just everyone goes to drama* (female, 14).

Upper class: *It's generally more like higher class persons that goes and sees that* (male, 18).

Dance

Older people: Older people I would have thought, rather than people my age (female, 15).

Females: Ballet will probably be maybe for girls, really girl types and posh (female, 15).

Classical Music

Upper class older people: It's usually upper class, middle age people with money to go and splash out every week on something like that (male, 17).

Enthusiasts: people having an interest in music (female, 15).

Heritage

Older people: Maybe middle aged sort of thing, if they are like at university or something like that, but I can't really see many kids going to them (male, 14).

Families: You get little kids going with their mum and dad (male, 16).

Apart from drama performances, the majority of interviewees were adamant that art/cultural events were 'not for young people, not for my age'. In effect the young people did not see themselves within this cultural world: and the perceived high profile and dominance of older people at such events in itself may constitute a barrier to future attendance. The association of cultural venues with affluence also resonated through the responses, while occasional reference was also made to arts audiences being made up of 'old-fashioned English people and people brought up on a farm', suggesting the absence of non-white and urban cultures.

As displayed below, when the sample were asked 'who would not go to such events, young people' was a constant response. Equally, the association of arts attendance with physical inactivity ('sitting still') and involving too little stimulation emerged as the young people defined non-attenders.

Who's not going to arts venues?

Visual Art

Young people: The young I would think, they would find it boring. It's got nothing ... [they'd say] 'let's go to a cinema' or somat, something that moves (female, 17).

Dance

Males: I'm sure they would probably be quite embarrassed to be sitting in the audience, it's definitely an image thing as well. They have just got to portray this image as being a tough man, so you watch the football instead (male, 18).

Physically active: People who can't sit still (female, 15).

Young people: It's not for teenagers, not young people at all (female, 15).

Drama

No experience: I think the only people that probably wouldn't be interested are people that have never actually been to see it before in their lives and don't really have an understanding of it (male, 18).

Non-arts: I think sport and science oriented people wouldn't really. It's all a bit too cultural for them I think (male, 18).

Heritage

Young people: I don't think many young people really go there as days out unless it's with the school or things like that, or if their parents are into it, but otherwise no, I don't that many people just there for a day out at our age (female, 14).

Music

Young people: I think young people. I have been to one in London once, and I just didn't understand it, and because it's not aimed towards young people, it can be off putting (male, 18).

A 15 year old boy, interviewed in London, offered a particularly powerful illustration of how the 'high' arts, in his eyes, were entirely divorced from today's modern culture. He was first asked to offer his thoughts on classical music and he responded with 'I am not really interested at all, not that music, no, it's not for me really'. He was then asked who it was for and replied '… it's for people that have been around longer. All this jazz and classical … it is classical, old, and it's like, *I am new*'. He went on to explain how it was a *'new way of life'* nowadays and while this new way of life did include high culture, it wasn't 'at the top of the pile'. Instead, pop music took precedence. One interesting aspect of his comments was the description of himself as a 'new' person, rather than a 'young' person. A strong sense of equivalence with adults and their high culture seems implicit in this answer. He was, in effect, defining himself as a new entity and as such in contrast, possibly in conflict, with an 'old' way of life. Such a perception, would no doubt affect the likelihood of attendance at events which were viewed as 'old' and for 'old people'. Equally, this construct of 'newness' might challenge established arts to consider and incorporate art forms such as video, computer art and the explosion of new music genres (hip-hop, jungle, drum and bass and so on). The cultural hybrid approach (as outlined in the previous chapter) would seem to require two-way and mutual recognition and respect.

4.3 ATTENDANCE ISSUES: LEVELS AND EXPERIENCES

4.3.1 Attendance levels

In order to ascertain the attendance habits of the sample, the young people were asked whether they had attended each of the five venue categories in the last month, in the last year or if ever. The table below summarises the results (responses were only recorded in one time category): show that the two most commonly visited venues were drama and heritage, while the least visited were dance venues.

	In the last month	In the last year	In the past	Total attendance	Never attended
Attendance Levels: An Audit					
Art	2	7	4	13	7
Dance	1	3	5	9	11
Drama	3	11	5	19	1
Music	2	1	9	12	8
Heritage	2	10	8	20	0

When asked which of the five categories they found least appealing and would not like to visit, dance again proved the least popular, nine of the sample stating they would not be attracted to dance events. Heritage venues were next most often nominated as not appealing (by 6 young people), followed by music (5), and then art (4). Just two young people were not interested in drama performances. The reasons given tended to be within a general 'refusenik' stance of 'I am just not into it, I just don't find it interesting'.

When the question about which type of venue they would most like to visit was posed, neither dance nor heritage received any mention. The most appealing venue was again the theatre, with nine interviewees expressing this preference. Art took second place with four nominations and three young people mentioned music events, although two were referring to popular music.

4.3.2 Attendance experiences

The young people were asked to recall a venue or event that they had visited in the last year for each of the cultural venue categories. Occasionally, where no attendance had occurred in the past year, they spoke of previous visits which they could remember well. Presented below are details of their attendance: who they went with, how the visit came about, how much it cost, any feelings about attending beforehand, the impressions of the events and lastly, any perceived effects, outcomes or gains.

Attendance experiences: reasons for visits

When interviewees were asked how their visits came about, a number of different sources were mentioned. Most commonly, reference was made to the attendance being school-related. Trips organised through school contact were mentioned by eight young people:

Drama   *Through one of my teachers at school. He said that it was being performed and I thought I would like to go and see it* (male, 18).

Heritage   *We went with school because we were doing it in history* (female, 15).

Peer-generated attendance i.e. visits arranged with and by friends were given as the impetus by seven young people. It is noteworthy that the idea of watching peers and friends perform seemed to give extra investment in the attendance in more than one instance:

Drama   *We knew* [a friend] *would be in it, so we all decided that it would be nice to go and see him* (female, 18).

Family-generated visits, suggested and organised by family members were mentioned in five cases.

Art   *Well my mum took us but my brother was kind of organising it, saying 'lets go!', because it was for him* (female, 14).

Impulse attendance, where the young people were serendipitously passing the venue concerned and took a spur of the moment decision to enter, was recalled by five interviewees:

Heritage   *It was kind of off the cuff again, we were just walking around and saw it, we hadn't even heard of the place* (male, 18).

Three mentioned *self-generated* visits, organised or chosen by the individual ('It was me actually, because I got a free pass from work'), while three referenced *advertising* arising through promotion of the venue or event, as the incentive for attendance:

Music   *It was advertised in the magazine and it was advertised outside the theatre and we walk past every day, so it caught my eye* (female, 15).

The cost of a ticket or entry fee ranged from free (as was the case with most art galleries) to £25 for a theatre seat. The young people were asked whether they considered this value for money. In all cases except one, they felt money had been well spent. This is noteworthy, as cost was cited as a frequent barrier to attendance in other studies, but the young people in this sample did not complain at the cost incurred when recalling examples of actual attendance. (The one individual who resented the cost had not wanted to attend the theatre from the outset.)

Prior to attending events, a number of interviewees recalled feelings of apprehension, and anticipated boredom. Such feelings of trepidation were particularly interesting, because their accounts very often showed that any negative outlook proved to be unjustified. Instead, the event was actually enjoyed. Typical comments included:

Dance   *I was a bit sceptical to start with, but I enjoyed it once I was there, it was good* (female, 15).

Art   *First of all, I thought it was going to be a bit boring. When I looked round it I knew I would be all right* (female, 18).

Drama   *I was thinking 'oh no!' … I was proved wrong* (male, 15).

Art   *I wasn't too thrilled with it to begin with, but yes, right up to the door, I didn't really want to go in* (male, 17).

Such apprehension, it could be argued, is the exact antithesis of gainful audience-mode. Many seasoned attenders at cultural events would see positive anticipation of a special occasion as a key component of the experience's pleasure. Making positive anticipation a feature of cultural events for young people is thus raised as an important issue.

Attendance experiences: positive and negative views

In giving their impressions of the actual events, young people spoke about aspects they particularly enjoyed and those that did not appeal. The range of perspectives and the discourse used was varied, and it was particularly noticeable that those who were low-level attenders simply had fewer comments and descriptors to offer about the cultural venues. The hit, buzz or excitement of the audience role was not articulated and hence, for them, in effect had not happened or been forgotten.

Art   *Just the different shapes of the statues really, I can't really remember* (female, 17).

Heritage   *I can't remember much, it was like your typical thing* (male, 15).

In contrast, other accounts of attendance recognised and gave particular emphasis to the fact that the experience had *exceeded expectations*. This discourse in effect, chose to recall and contrast the original negative apprehension factor with positive outcomes. However a key question might be, does this negative anticipation still militate against high impact? Equally, the relationship between vague/non-specific accounts of the event and low-level impact may be worth further exploration.

For indeed, at the opposite extreme were those young people who could articulate and convey the intense *physical power and presence* of their arts audience experience. Others noted the positive experience of *audience membership:* the notion of belonging, participating and joining in. The recollection of events as generally pleasurable and fun was another response, with this enjoyment factor being specifically related to *interactive* and hands-on possibilities in some instances.

Attendance experiences: positive views

Exceeding expectations

Art *It was better than I thought it would be, I enjoyed it a lot more* (female, 14).

Drama *I thought it was really good, it was much better than doing it in school* (female, 15).

Drama *I thought it would be very boring, but it wasn't really that boring* (male, 14).

Heritage *It was better than what I thought it was going to be because it was quite big and I thought it looked interesting* (male, 18).

Heritage *It was different, I really enjoyed it when I really thought I wouldn't, but yes it was good* (female, 17).

Art *A lot of it I was impressed by. A lot of it I sort of went 'I don't really get that' but I remember just looking at the sculpture as well and photographs and things and I just generally enjoyed it. I thought it was really good and I had to get dragged out in the end* (male, 18).

Fun/enjoyment/interactive

Drama *They used so many different styles and stuff and it was just so funny. It was just really funny and it made me laugh and I came out feeling better than I did when I went in* (male, 18).

Drama *It was really good, because I love pantomimes. They are a good laugh* (female, 14).

Art *The gallery had sections for all ages ... like little board games for children ... and computer games for them as well* (female, 14).

Heritage *It was good, everyone enjoyed it because it was just interesting, it wasn't one of these places you go and get bored, there's things to do, it's all interactive, hands-on stuff* (male, 16).

Heritage *I thought the moving dinosaurs were quite good. They have got these dinosaurs that actually respond to the humans that are there* (male, 16).

Audience membership/participation

Drama *Everyone just having fun and everyone is just like loud and all ages are there as well, there's like little children and there's old people and everyone is just happy* (female, 14).

Drama *It was amazing. It got the whole audience involved, they talked to the audience and it was so lively, dancing and there's singing, it was very good* (female, 15).

Drama *They kept coming out of the play to speak to you, the actually were saying to you 'all right?' and 'how is this to you' and you actually felt like you were part of it* (male, 18).

Drama *Good atmosphere, everybody is there to enjoy it, so it was good* (female, 17).

Physical, presence/power of arts experience

Art *It was just so interesting and like the way it was set up and you could go round, you could sit on things, you could look at it … it was just like everywhere you looked there was something interesting, so that really appeals to the eye. It's not like an art gallery where you just go through and look at pictures on the wall. That has actually got the sculptures there and you can look at everything really closely* (female, 18).

Music *It was again, amazing. It was like feeling it, if you listen to it on a tape, which is what I have been lumbered with sometimes at home, you just listen to it and go 'no, that's really not that good'. But when you go there you can feel the music* (female, 15).

While most of the visits were rated positively by the sample, a few negative comments also emerged. The accounts of negative experiences of arts events generally covered three major issues (and ones that recur in other accounts of barriers). As the interview extracts below show, the sample referred to a *lack of understanding* of the content; to a sense of alienation from the *ambience* (e.g. feeling conspicuous, out of place in an environment for 'old' people) and to a rejection of the actual *content*.

Attendance experiences: negative views

Lack of understanding and confusion

Art *I don't mind Da Vinci or modern art, but some modern art is just really weird. I don't understand it* (female, 15).

Art *A lot of it I sort of went 'I don't really get that'* (male, 18).

Heritage *It was really difficult, there weren't many signs or anything telling* *you where to go for certain things, it was really big as well, it wasn't as inter-esting as I thought it would be because everything was scattered around and I couldn't find what I was looking for* (male, 17).

Ambience

Art *The layout was a bit plain, the pictures were really interesting but they were kind of just lined up and you just walked along and everyone stood and read, looked and walked on* (female, 14).

Drama *The atmosphere was really dead there was a lot of older people there and me and my cousin were like shoved in with all of them* (female, 17).

Drama *The atmosphere of the theatre is good as well, as long as there's not too many old people... you don't feel able to be yourself if there's loads of like other people looking at you* (female, 14).

Heritage *I think if you go at this sort of age and you just like walk around then you are really looked down on by all the old people like 'oh you are not meant to be in here', sort of a bit cagey towards you* (female, 14).

Content

Dance *The only problem is ballet, they tend to go on and on, I really liked it, I didn't mind sitting through like two or three hours of it, but I can imagine some people getting really bored about it* (female, 15).

4.3.3 Effects of cultural attendance

The young people were asked if they had 'gained' anything from their visits and audience experiences and whether or not they were more or less likely to attend similar venues in the future. Six types of effect emerged:

- a more positive attitude towards the arts and culture;
- reinforced appreciation of the arts;
- motivation to attend future events;
- acquisition of knowledge through attendance;
- psychological well-being as a consequence of arts consumption;
- inspiration to participate in the arts.

Through attendance, some of the young people realised that the arts and culture were not as boring as first thought, thus the visit had instilled more positive attitudes:

Art   *Other ones I had been to had been a bit boring and I just found out that they weren't all that boring, not all of them* (female, 14).

Music   *Probably a slightly better perception of it than before, maybe slightly encouraged me a bit* (male, 17).

For those already won over by the value of attendance, a positive experience served to reinforce their enjoyment of the arts.

Drama *Apart from the memories, an even greater enjoyment of the theatre* (female, 15).

Music *It made me even more interested in music* (female, 15).

Some specifically volunteered that attendance had encouraged them to want to go to similar events:

Dance *It made me want to go and see more of them* (female, 14).

Heritage *I would go back there again, because it was good and I would like to go to other houses* (female, 17).

When asked directly, the vast majority felt they would like to visit cultural venues again. Thus, once the young people actually experienced a cultural event, the outcome was largely positive. There were only two incidences of visits where the individuals concerned said they wouldn't go again and in both cases, it was to a particular play or a particular museum, rather than theatres or museums in general:

Heritage *It hasn't put me off, it's put me off that museum in particular. Like I wouldn't tell anyone, if someone said I am going to the … what do you think of it? I would say 'it's not stunning'* (male, 17).

However, it is worth emphasising that despite a new found willingness to assume an audience role, just two individuals could actually report follow-up attendance since the visits they described. The idea that a positive experience equates with and ensures further attendance is thus perhaps challenged: certainly, further research into 'the return factor' may be a beneficial line of enquiry.

Nine young people recognised the educational outcomes of attendance: they felt 'better informed' and in some cases, the experience assisted their learning at school.

Heritage *I learnt a lot about the history of the place and about history in general, about the period. It's a Victorian house and Victorians copied a lot from other periods, so you learn a lot about all the different periods from the house, it was good* (female, 15).

Drama *A good mark in my English essay. Before we were only reading a book and I find it quite hard to picture what it's going to be like, so it's better if you can see it* (male, 14).

Drama *It helped in my theatre studies work because we picked up on the style and used it in things that we did* (male, 18).

A number of young people's accounts referenced pleasure and enjoyment as an outcome and how they had felt good as a consequence of their attendance, most notably in the category of drama.

Drama   *It was just really funny and it made laugh and I came out feeling*
         better than I did when I went in (male, 18).

Drama   *I don't know if I gained anything from going, I don't know really,*
         I just really enjoyed it (female, 17).

Drama   *Just a good experience, I think it was just fun* (female, 14).

Finally, among two high attenders, the experience of attendance had inspirational outcomes. One girl now wished to pursue a career as an artist and visits to galleries had provided lots of ideas. Another girl, who had attended a performance by her 'personal hero', Evelyn Glenny, was encouraged to take her performing more seriously.

Art   *Sort of inspiration to try things out and I think a lot of inspiration to*
         become an artist just a wider view of art (female, 14).

Music   *It has re-sparked my interest in the music ... I have been playing per-*
         cussion for three years, and that started me starting grades and things
         (female, 15).

In among the reported effects, there were eight incidences where the young people felt they had *not* gained anything from their visits.

4.4 ATTENDING A VENUE: A CULTURAL CONVERSION

One of the twenty interviewees provided a striking example of conversion to the arts, and that it was possible, through a positive experience, to challenge preconceived notions of what the arts are like and stimulate attendance at future exhibitions. Equally, the story perhaps challenges notions that art is only 'caught' from other people (Harland et al.,1995): it is certainly a timely reminder that the quality of the arts encountered also has considerable import.

This 18 year old began by describing a recent visit to a national gallery in London, which began with apprehension. However, the paintings were so impressive that he seemed truly won over and opened up to art. At the same time, his commentary points to factors which obstructed attendance, namely misconceptions concerning cost, lack of understanding, the quietness of galleries, feeling out of place and attendance discomfort/anomie.

An interview extract

Feelings beforehand

Q   *Was it your idea to go to the gallery?*
A   No, it was hers really, my sister and American pen pal.

Q *How did you feel about that suggestion then?*

A I wasn't too thrilled with it to begin with, but yes, right up to the door, I didn't really want to go in.

Q *Why was that?*

A I don't know, because art has never really interested me because I have never been any good at it myself, so haven't really related to people that are good at it, haven't thought about it.

Q *Did it cost anything to go to the gallery?*

A No it was free, which was a bit of a plus.

Q *Were you surprised by that?*

A Yes, I was, I was very shocked, because it's a huge place and I thought they must need some funding, but it's obviously government funded and donations.

Impressions

Q *OK. So you weren't too keen beforehand and then you went in, you had a look around, so what did you think of it then?*

A It was really overwhelming, some of the pictures were like huge massive and they were like really majestic and they just trapped you in them, really it was an experience.

Q *So was it mainly the art that you were impressed with or anything else ...?*

A Just the art really and the size of the building. The building itself was really cool as well.

Q *So you say the art was massive, was there anything else that really stood out and grabbed your attention and made you feel, 'this is quite good really'?*

A No, just all the pictures, and the emotions in the pictures and you could see what the artists were thinking and I never really related to it that much, because when I drew a picture, I just drew a picture, you could see that there was like feeling went into their pictures.

Q *How did it compare to your expectations then?*

A It was a hell of a lot better than I thought it would be.

Conversion with a caveat

Q *Do you think that now you have been there you are more likely to go to other art galleries?*

A Yes, definitely.

Q   *What do you think you have gained from that trip then, generally?*

A   Opened my mind up to art basically, which made me want to go more, because again I was kind of roped into going, I had no choice, but if I had had the choice I still would never have gone and would still be saying it really didn't interest me, so that's how I think it is for many young people, you have to be forced to go and then you will get into it.

Q   *But is there anything else that you think you could change about art galleries … anything at all that could make it better for young people?*

A   Yes, well the main part where all the pictures of Jesus were, it was like kind of bland as it had the quietness, everyone was quiet and it had the medieval smell, and so you go in there and you are kind of like intimidated by all the paintings and you want to get out as quickly as you can, but in the Icons of Pop one, it was like really more relaxed and it was like more [modern], and so that's generally what I think young people today would want, is like a more modern environment.

Q   *Would you say you actually did feel uncomfortable in the older section?*

A   Yes, because it was only like me and this American pen pal just walking around, everyone else was like really old and they were talking about the artist and so on, 'I have seen his work before', and I was just standing there looking really naïve and ignorant, [saying] 'yes it's a cool painting'.

This individual managed to 'cross the line' despite his reservations. The reality of attendance proved to be enjoyable, but at the same time, negative factors such as a perceived lack of understanding and feeling out of place still came to light. Interviews with the rest of the sample identified many more factors which could affect the chances of attendance and these will be addressed in the following section.

4.5 BARRIERS TO ATTENDANCE: INHIBITING FACTORS

Throughout the interviews, young people mentioned factors which seemed to deter their attendance at arts and cultural venues. Six major types of factor emerged:

- *Event factors:* including both venue issues (e.g. the location, cost of attending, lack of publicity, timing), and issues relating to the actual content (e.g. lack of visual interest, length of performance).
- *Personal factors:* not having the time to attend, not having anyone to

go with, feeling conspicuous, embarrassed or uncomfortable when attending, and lacking the understanding to fully appreciate the event.

- *School factors:* not receiving sufficient encouragement to attend, no opportunities to attend and being turned off the arts by particular lessons.
- *Family factors:* enforced attendance, overexposure to the arts, or lack of interest in the family.
- *Peer factors:* friends who are not interested in the arts, friends who have other interests and the need to maintain an image in the peer group.
- *Media and image factors:* negative images of art and culture in the media.

4.5.1 Event factors

In this category, geographical location of venues in relation to the homes of young people, ranked as the highest nomination for non-attendance, followed by perceived costs; lack of information; and timing of the event.

The sample selection had deliberately endeavoured to interview young people from both rural and urban locations. However, despite of their proximity to large towns and cities, 12 of the young people felt that where they lived did detrimentally affect their access to arts and culture. It is worth noting that the 'territories' within which young people circulate are generally quite small, restricted by a reliance on public transport and limited finances. Hence, even a relatively short distance for an adult traveller could present genuine difficulties for teenage audiences. One interviewee explained the specific problems of living in a village:

You have to get your mum and dad to drive you, you have to get on the bus which is quite expensive, even just to go quite a short way, so you sort of have to work out all the times and everything, so that can be quite hard, so I think living in a village area is quite hard if you want to go out for the night (female, 14).

Even moving around a major city was perceived as difficult, and, combined with expense, prohibited attendance.

It costs four quid to get there and then it costs on top of that what you have to pay to get in, the drinks and all the rest of it. Yes, it's also the transport systems are absolutely terrible in London … It's a whole number of factors, by the end of it, if you add them up, you just go 'sod it' (male, 18).

I live in the sticks so there's no way I can get anywhere. Fifteen, 20 minute walk to the train stations which isn't too bad, but then you have got to get a tube to somewhere, and that really takes you into the centre of London, unless you want to start changing lines and go off in different directions (male, 17).

The cost of travelling to the event and paying to get in, was the second most commonly cited factor impacting on attendance.

Probably worrying about the money, how much it's going to cost, I haven't actually phoned up and asked, but I imagine [such events] *would be quite expensive to get into* (male, 18).

Inner city prices for a start are really big and also, for young people, they don't really have that much money floating about, so it's a bit difficult (male, 18).

The third most common factor cited as a barrier to attendance was a lack of awareness, stemming from a sense of insufficient or inappropriate publicity around arts and cultural venues. Either there was not enough advertising of these events, or what advertising there was, did not target the youth market:

Drama   *I don't know where to go to, to see what's on and how much it is* (male, 14).

Dance   *I would like to go and see it again, but I just don't know where any are on, I don't really know about that many* (female, 14).

Music   *I don't really hear about many orchestras and stuff like that going on* (male, 17).

Music   *I have always wanted to get into jazz, but I just don't hear enough about it* (male, 16).

Finally, in terms of 'macro' event factors, a few interviewees commented that their attendance had been prohibited due to the timing of the event:

Drama   *Sometimes they are only held on specific days and they are normally during the week, like on a Wednesday night and it's like 'well I can't get into Leeds on a Wednesday night and I won't be home until like half eleven' and there's no way I would be able to get up in the morning, so that's normally why I can't go* (female, 14).

Beyond the accessibility issue, some of the sample again referred to micro factors: the intrinsic content as a barrier. A specific 'turn off' associated with classical concerts, for instance, was the lack of visual interest. One interviewee felt that orchestras were 'just unattractive, you have got to sit there for ages in an uncomfortable seat, with the tiniest pair of binoculars, viewing some bald fellow with a cello'. Dance, drama and music were criticised for being overly long at times, making it difficult to enjoy the performance. Another interviewee contrasted the arrangement at jazz clubs:

If you are at a classical music concert or something, you can't really talk, you just have to sit there and watch … It's a long time just to expect them to sit there and do nothing and with jazz, my image of a jazz club where you can sit and drink, that's more appealing, the social bit (male, 16).

The issue of entrance to the unfamiliar surfaced again. The venue was perceived as unwelcoming, uninteresting and even intimidating, the likelihood of making those steps and 'crossing the line' thus diminished. One 17 year old girl who was quite keen to visit her local art gallery, was genuinely deterred by its appearance:

> It's so ... I just ... like, Leeds art gallery and that... two doors and 'Oh God I don't want to go in, I am a bit scared' ... like, there's no colours, there's no nothing.

Again with respect to art galleries, one interviewee explained that art is not displayed in places that young people 'see or hold with any great respect or esteem' (male, 17).

Put together, the sample again highlights the qualities of arts and cultural events that affect young people adversely. Lack of familiarity with the ambience and protocols of arts events; lack of social opportunity; a content that lacks appeal to more than one receptor/intelligence (e.g. no visual interest at classical concerts, no sound or movement in galleries); and challenges to young people's physical and mental stamina (e.g. sitting still on uncomfortable seats or having to concentrate for too long) all feature in these accounts.

4.5.2 Personal factors

The second set of barriers were located within the personal preferences or psyche of prospective arts consumer.

The most common personal factor influencing attendance was 'not having the time' to engage in such things. One interviewee was really involved in sport, so everything else took second place. In other instances, the consequence of working was noted:

> I don't really have time to go. I work every day and I work on a Saturday and on a Sunday. I just don't do anything really (female, 17).

Attendance at college and on training courses was also thought to reduce the amount of available spare time. A 15 year old girl who was currently with a training provider studying hairdressing, explained how she was 'busier now, because I am just working and then coming home really. I don't like doing anything really when I get home'. A fellow trainee also felt she was busier but conceded that if she did have the time, then she still probably would not go to any arts and cultural venues. Choice and preference in how to use leisure time, was thus significant.

> I think as you get older the appeal of the place goes down a bit because you don't see it as exciting ... [there's no] buzz of the theatre any more as you get older, because you think 'oh I could be doing something else, going out' (female, 14).

The notion of 'going out' here intimates certain adolescent social and leisure imperatives which arts events did not seem to fulfil.

Three interviewees complained that they had no one to go with:

I haven't got the guts to go on my own, I just don't want to go on my own, I want someone to come with me (female, 17).

I wouldn't go on my own, I would want to go with somebody else, but if my friends aren't involved, I am not really as keen (male, 16).

The need for company suggests two possibilities: that some young people require leisure pursuits which are essentially sociable and socially acceptable or they simply find the prospect of attendance slightly unnerving and therefore prefer company for support. This phenomenon of 'attendance discomfort' was expressed more explicitly by other interviewees. Interestingly, they were high attenders but they still felt out of place and, at times, conspicuous. They often attributed this to a dissonant physical appearance: e.g. casual attire at a formal evening and being a young person in among a predominately more mature audience. The sense of 'exclusion' is particularly telling in these instances.

Drama *I think if you go at this sort of age and you just like run around then you are really looked down on by all the old people like 'oh you are not meant to be in here', sort of a bit cagey towards you* (female, 14).

Music *I remember going against it and going in combat trousers, just for the fun of it. You felt really out of place, everyone just looked at you.* (male, 17).

A couple of young people however admitted that attendance at arts and cultural events could be 'embarrassing' in relation to potential exclusion from their own peer group.

I would like to listen to some of that stuff, but you really couldn't be caught dead going to see it (male, 18).

When I was younger it was like you couldn't say you were going to the opera because it was really uncool. You just looked like a gimp if you went, but now I can imagine that I would (male, 17).

A final personal factor inhibiting attendance which was frequently mentioned, particularly in relation to art galleries, revolved around a lack of understanding of the art form.

I always think 'oh I am out of my depth, I don't understand it' (female, 18).

It's lack of knowledge that puts people off, 'cos paintings are often abstract and as a viewer, you need to know what you are looking at (male, 18).

The following interview extract, where the respondent had attended an exhibition of his sister's art work at college, shows how both ambience and explanation can enhance appreciation of the arts experience.

Access to the arts

> Young person: *I can remember it was in, like a tent, and then there was like surface on the ground with a lot of paintings around with different students and* **the students were going around with their paintings and describing what they mean and stuff like that.**

> Interviewer: Could you compare it to other art galleries you have been to, was it different at all do you think?

> Young person*: It was a more updated version, it was like people were acting in a different way. Like if you see them in other art galleries, they are taking notes of the work and trying to figure out themselves ...* [at the exhibition] **everything was getting explained to you as you were walking past so you would know.**

> Interviewer: Did that make any difference to you at all?

> Young person*: It made it easier to understand because some of the stuff ... because you have got art work that's different and* **it means something and you wouldn't know unless it was explained.**

4.5.3 School factors

The comments made by some of the interviewees suggested that school could be a negative factor affecting attendance. However, it is important to note that overall, school presented far more examples of facilitating attendance, and this positive association will be addressed in the Section 4.6.

In the first instance, seven interviewees thought school had not properly emphasised the arts: there was simply a lack of encouragement. An 'A' level theatre studies student had detected disapproval from non-arts teachers whom he felt did not see theatre studies as 'a proper A level' and implied that visits to the theatre took up 'valuable homework time'. Another keen performing arts student, felt the art department had been 'down played at school', with more emphasis on academic subjects, such as science and maths.

Music   *They have got to be taught in school, because at our school we haven't really been taught that much about music. We have been taught how to play it, but not really about the other side of it* (male, 16).

As well as failing to promote or give equal status to arts and culture, some young people felt they had not been provided with the opportunities to attend cultural events:

> *I think* [school] *has an influence because it doesn't really give you the opportunities to go to them* (female, 14).

> *I have never really been made to do much art and never really been made to look into art, so I have never ... it's never been exposed to me* (male, 17).

In keeping with earlier research (Harland et al., 1995), a couple of interviewees felt that certain arts lessons and teachers had actually 'turned them off' the arts. In one example, a high attender recollected how music lessons used to be 'fun' at primary age '... at little school ... you got tinkering around on like little xylophones and making up music'. At secondary school, music had become more technical: 'you are going too deep into it' and, perhaps more significantly, musical appreciation was turned into a literacy task. The consequence was that motivation to attend classical music concerts really 'went down':

> *I think what's affected me most is my school, because I had music, I was forced to sit for hours with my friends, as my music teacher just used to play us bits of music and make us write down about them and that's why everyone hated music lessons and that's why I gave it up* (female, 14).

At the other end of the spectrum, a very low-level attender associated arts and culture directly and solely with school, given that most of her attendance had arisen through mandatory school trips. The fact that the two were intricately intertwined meant that now she had left school, she wished to 'leave all that behind ... get school out of my head'.

4.5.4 Family factors

Interviewees could cite factors within the family which either had put them off attending, prevented attendance or more commonly, had 'no influence' simply because there was no tradition of visiting arts and cultural events.

Being put off, in one instance, was ascribed to a dad who played a lot of jazz music, leading to a dislike of jazz. In another instance, enforced attendance, whereby a respondent recollected being 'dragged round' museums, which had a 'negative effect'. On the other hand, one 15 year old girl had wanted to attend drama productions when she was little but was prevented from doing so, because her parents thought she 'wouldn't understand'. Another boy, aged 16, from a large family explained that they didn't go to places so much due to cost and different interests within the family. When asked if families affected attendance, a number of interviewees often responded along the lines of 'no, they are not into art', or 'no, they are not interested in that sort of thing'. Although not directly preventing attendance, lack of enthusiasm within the family, appeared to transfer to the child in some instances.

4.5.5 Peer-group factors

When interviewees described their attendance experiences, most recollected that the visits took place in the presence of peers. Hence, a lack of interest among peers or at least a different set of interests, reduced the frequency of visits to cultural venues. The consequences, as already noted, were that the young person had no one to go with or, if they did go, their attendance might elicit disapproving comments from friends. Image within the peer group was sometimes threatened by partaking in 'less cool' activities:

My family takes me a lot [to concerts], *but my friends are a bit uninterested, so I think that has, if anything, a negative effect, because you can be put off by what your friends think* (female, 15).

Attendance at dance, especially ballet, was cited as a particular stumbling block for males:

I am sure they would probably be quite embarrassed to be sitting in the audience. It's definitely an image thing as well. They have just got to portray this image of being a tough man, so you watch the football instead (male, 18).

Another interviewee, whose favourite subject was PE, felt that his friends preferred him to 'concentrate' on sports:

Some of friends have, they told me, not necessarily told me, but concentrate on my sports instead of stuff like that (male, 15).

Lastly, one girl explained that her friends were more into Indian music and they 'don't like English music'. The result was that none of her friends would go to classical concerts and she felt she couldn't go on her own. The specific challenge of exchange and 'crossing the line' between different cultures is perhaps raised here. Overall, however, peer influence and peer pressure, clearly did affect these young people's inclination and opportunity to attend places of art and culture.

4.5.6 Images of attendance

Given that arts and cultural attendance was often limited and sometimes non-existent among the sample, views were also influenced by other sources. For instance, one interviewee believed that art galleries were 'so quiet', but then realised she had never actually been to one. When asked 'where have you got this idea that they are quiet places?' she replied:

Television I think, the way they portray it on the television, on the comedies and stuff … It's portrayed as quite boring I think. They seem to take the mickey out of it, that it's so quiet, boring and sedate. (female, 15).

Another interviewee felt that art work in books was 'down sized' and therefore less impressive:

You look at a book and the painting just looks like someone has drawn like lots of lines on paper and it's like not the same feeling that you get when you actually go and see it in kind of the flesh. It's like shrunken down and put on

a glass paper, it's not the same as it is on the canvas, hung up, full size
(male, 17).

Thus, the image, the stereotype and lack of first-hand experience all appear to act as attendance barriers and suggest a strong PR role for arts organisations and schools in challenging young people's preconceptions.

4.6 FACTORS FACILITATING ATTENDANCE

What is it that actually persuades young people to 'cross the line' and walk through the entrances of theatres, art galleries and museums? Who, or what, is perceived to be creating the conditions which allow young people to engage positively in a consumer role?

When the 20 young people were questioned about this, four major types of facilitating factor emerged :

- *Family factors:* opportunities and encouragement from the family, interest within the family and arts role models.
- *School factors:* attendance opportunities, encouragement from particular teachers.
- *Peer factors:* encouragement from friends, and attendance when supporting friends who perform in the arts.
- *Media factors:* interest raised through arts coverage in the media.

4.6.1 Family factors

Interviewees described how their families influenced attendance in one of three ways. Firstly, families provided the opportunity to visit arts and cultural venues. Secondly, they recognised a general encouragement within the family and thirdly, there were particular family members who appeared, through their own involvement in the arts, to generate enthusiasm and interest in the young person.

Maternal influence upon arts appreciation (Harland et al., 1995) also surfaced. A high attender of dance performances, explained 'that's what my family are into doing, my mum loves ballet and I love ballet as well and dance, we just go and see things' (female, 14). Similarly, an avid art fan, confirmed that her family had 'definitely' affected her attendance because 'my mum is really into art … so my whole family are very arty'. Over the years, she had been taken to exhibitions and subsequently developed an interest herself.

Other family role models emerged as well. The sole lover of classical music within the sample had been very influenced by her father, a conductor of a well-known girls choir, 'My dad is very musical, he enjoys going to see the same sorts of things as I do' and as a result her attendance had developed over the years:

I have always been quite interested in music from a very young age and that's got a lot to do with my dad being interested in the same things. It has developed a lot as I have got older, the sorts of things I have gone to see have changed, become a lot more varied (female, 15).

Another interviewee had been inspired by his brother whose art work was scattered around the house. 'Before, I didn't really take too much of an interest in it. When I started seeing his stuff I just thought "yes, this is really good" and took a really big interest it' (male, 18). Being in close proximity to such individuals clearly lead to an osmosis of interest, caught from one family member to another. All but one of the young people in the category of high attendance spoke of an individual in the family who was very keen on the arts.

4.6.2 School factors

Overall, school was cited most as a key factor in encouraging attendance.

First and foremost, school succeeded in placing young people into museums, art galleries and theatres. Among the low-level attenders, school had been the main reason for their attendance:

I don't think I would have gone if I wasn't at school (female, 17).

I haven't been taken to any with my parents, but the school just lets you know about them (female, 15).

One 15 year old boy felt that school had the 'biggest impact of all'. Before a school visit, he recollected considering 'I am not going to come into school that day', but 'you do come [to school] and you do go and it's really interesting'. This comment perhaps underlines the importance of 'taster' attendance which schools are able to provide.

Like role models within the family, young people also mentioned individual teachers at school or FE college who had enthused them. Again the resonances with previous research are apparent:

It's really different like at college. It's just kind of [the teacher] *says 'Do you want to go to the theatre?' and we all say yes, and he gets us cheap tickets and we go together* (female, 17).

I think [school] *has helped yes, especially ... well it's probably last year that it influenced me the most because of the teacher I had, but I am not really as keen now because she has left ... she was like a role model in art for me* (male, 14).

Influence of school? *I think it's probably had a fair bit over the years, during lower school, doing drama and then drama GCSE and then performing art, they do encourage you to go, drama teachers do* (male 18).

As an outcome of attendance through school incidences of interest being raised were cited. Trips organised through school made some young people realise that places like museums and the theatre can actually be quite entertaining and in accordance, their attitudes towards these places had improved: 'I mean they probably made me think "yes, they are not such a bad place as I thought they were going to be"'.

> *There was a chance to go on a trip on a Saturday and you could choose to go and there was quite a high attendance for that, so it obviously has improved interest in things like that* (female, 14).

However, sometimes just enjoying the subject itself was enough to encourage attendance:

> *Because I have done history at GCSE and I have learnt more about it and when I have got the opportunity then I would go to a museum just to see … because I have learnt about the history … to actually see history and it's cool, isn't it. Seeing dead bodies and stuff, I don't know why, just lots of bones* (male, 17).

Interviewees who took arts-related subjects such as music, drama and performing arts, particularly felt that their courses had facilitated attendance:

> *Mainly for the course that I am studying, means that I have to go. They don't force you to go, but it helps, but I think when I finish the course, I am still going* [to go] (male, 18).

Within the descriptions of attendance, interviewees specifically stated they went because they thought it would help them with their school work. This was the case even among the low-level attenders. One girl went to an art gallery on her own, to get ideas for an art exam, another low attender went to the theatre to see a GCSE text acted out on stage:

> *I thought it would like help me with my GCSEs because we were studying it at the time, so I thought I would learn a lot more about it, so we were reading the book, so I thought well, if we had read the book and then I had seen the play then I would know a lot more about it* (female, 17).

At the very least, studying an arts subject served to keep related venues and events on the minds of young people. One interviewee whose attendance at heritage venues had gone down explained:

> *I don't do history anymore and it's like … it's just taken my mind off it* (male, 15).

Nevertheless, as the previous section showed, if attendance was too heavily linked with school work, there was a danger that the enjoyment and entertainment factor may be lost.

4.6.3 Peer-group factors

There were six examples where young people felt that enthusiasm and encouragement within their peer group had promoted attendance 'All my friends are into it, so that's cool, a lot of encouragement there' (male, 18).

There were also examples where having friends who were directly involved as arts performers encouraged attendance, because of the wish to show support:

With my friends being in plays, that made me go more (female, 18).

My friend is a dancer, so we used to go and see her in shows and things (female, 17).

4.6.4 Media factors

While images in the media could be detrimental to attendance, three young people felt that TV footage had actually fuelled their interest. One person was now quite keen to visit an art gallery and another two had seen River Dance performed, introducing them to the world of dance. However, very significantly none of the interviewees who cited this influence had actually achieved attendance.

Origins of high attendance

The young people who were high attenders were each asked how they first became interested in venues. The interest originated from a number of sources:

It's a family thing

Two interviewees explained that their high attendance was because from an early age, their families had taken them to arts and cultural venues and these experiences had laid the foundations for future attendance:

When I was a child my mum used to take me to BFG and things like that in the Grand and things, and I liked them when I was little. Then, just as I have got older, I have gone and seen lots of different types of things being performed (female, 14).

Another 14 year old girl who was especially interested in art and natural history explained that she was taken to 'so many when [she] was younger' and she 'knew what they were like'. Frequency of attendance thus led to a familiarisation with these places, including their ambience and protocols, which in the long run, she felt, made it much easier to visit such venues. Indeed, this interviewee described a cumulative effect in that 'going to so many just made me want to go to more'.

School sparks interest

Two interviewees cited school as a predominant influence underpinning their high attendance. One 17 year old girl who studied history at school found it 'quite interesting to know where famous people had lived'. Similarly, an 18 year boy reported that English was his favourite subject and a good English teacher 'sort of encouraged me ... she kept on telling me about these plays coming to the National and things like that, so I try and go down and see them'.

Participation encourages attendance

One clear correlation to emerge from the high attenders was that those who participated in the arts were also likely to attend cultural venues. One girl had danced as a child and as a result, dance had 'always been brought to my attention'. The same girl, joined a choir at the age of ten bringing her into contact with musical people and introducing her to the concert scene. This involvement was thought to have had 'a vast influence'. Another A level theatre studies student traced his attendance origins to a youth theatre he joined as a child:

> Sort of started going to a youth theatre thing when I was probably about ten, and I did a musical then, so from about then onwards (male, 18).

Career pursuit

The same high attender who mentioned the encouragement of an English teacher reflected that he had increased his theatre visits in order to pursue a career in performing arts. It is worth noting therefore that attendance can stem from a number of interacting sources, rather than a single defining moment or particular individual:

> I suppose its a career thing, that I want to get into that sort of field. So I kind of said 'right, you go out and research it' really, and I have enjoyed it (male, 18).

Peer influence

One high attender cited his friends as an influence, but also felt that interest had been generated through his involvement in drama productions which enlightened him as to the complexities of performance and all that goes on backstage.

> I would say friends urged you on sometimes or like you get invited and just go and see it (male, 15).

A break from the norm

Finally, one 18 year old boy cited his own personal motivation as the reason for high attendance 'I just wanted to get out of my tedious life and get acting myself'. Through his acting, he became increasingly interested and therefore wanted to see how other people acted.

4.7 STRATEGIES FOR IMPROVING ATTENDANCE

The previous section highlighted those factors capable of facilitating or hindering attendance and as such confirms other research findings outlined in Chapter 1. While is important to take note again of these influences, this project chose also to consult young people directly, with regards to what 'they' thought could be done to improve attendance. Hence the specific recommendations made by the 20 interviewees for making cultural venues 'more appealing' to young people are now presented. Interviewees were asked what sort of cultural events they wanted to encounter, what would appeal to them and what could make the arts 'attractive'. Their recommendations – varied and insightful – matched the kinds of initiative outlined in the previous chapter. In total, 11 suggestions were made:

- art galleries and museums should become increasingly 'interactive'
- improvements to the advertising of events and venues
- promotion of the arts and culture through school
- a socialisation of the arts, through add-ons such as cafes and leisure facilities
- shorter performances
- a modernisation of arts and culture
- cheaper tickets and special offers for young people
- performances by young people
- portraying issues which matter to young people
- relocating the arts to venues familiar to young people
- providing opportunities to experience the arts

4.7.1 Going interactive

Both art galleries and heritage were seen as relatively 'static'. One boy described an art gallery as, 'smooth and slow'. Recommendations for improvement generally centred around making these venues increasingly 'interactive', with an injection of movement, sound and opportunities for participation.

Another suggestion was to enact battle scenes at castles: 'I would love to go and see that, a proper war going on in a castle' (male, 18). One girl felt galleries should be made more alive and suggested using guides who could explain the art on view 'and be dressed up in the style of a Picasso'. A budding architect suggesting modifying the building, moving away from the traditional white walled, square rooms, instead creating atmospheric conditions, through the use of colour and irregular dimensions.

> I think I would have people in costumes and just have people walking round the house, not so much showing you round, but just people walking round the house. You could just stop and talk to them and they will just stop and tell you about the house, that would be good (female, 15).

Not only did the interviewees advocate interactive venues, they also offered an explanation for this approach. A 17 year old boy preferred historic houses to museums because the latter removed the artefacts from their natural or historical surroundings. Another interviewee made a similar observation:

> When you go to a stately home you feel like you are actually there, as if a character could walk in through the door. In museums, everything's like on boards and things (female, 15).

One 17 year old boy, recognised the learning opportunities to be derived from interactive displays. Thinking back to his early school days, he recalled that you 'enjoy learning more doing things yourself, something coming about through you discovering it rather than just being told "look at that"'. He then compared static displays with being told to copy out of a book, neither of which was particularly engaging.

4.7.2 More advertising, better advertising, advertising for young people

For all five categories of venue, young people suggested improvements to the advertising of events. In the first instance, the interviewees recommended more advertising to raise awareness. With respect to art galleries, one interviewee explained that most people believe they have to pay admission charges, when in actual fact they are often free. This misconception was confirmed in interviews with other young people.

Others felt advertising was not specifically targeted at the youth market:

> It is aimed at quite an older age group. The posters are very mature I would say, so I think if it was aimed more at a young audience you might get a young audience. I would say, more aim it at the young people because the advertising is aimed very much at adults (female, 15).

A 15 year old boy felt advertising did not adequately convey the content of cultural events. He compared theatre advertising with posters for films and felt the high profile of films meant that young people were generally informed about what they are going to see and would have an idea of the story-line beforehand, following coverage in magazines and TV promos. In his view, drama productions did not receive the same youth media attention and consequently, 'you are not going to go and watch something that you don't know what it's going to be like'.

Lastly, advertising needed to be engaging, capable of capturing the interest of young people. One interviewee cited the example of the West End production, *Chicago*. 'The posters' sort of stood out and you have just got to grab people's attention and say "you will enjoy this, come and see it"'.

4.7.3 Promotion through schools

The idea that dance and drama could be promoted through schools was voiced. One interviewee, who had experience of theatre in education, felt the same principle could be applied to dance, by bringing in dance companies. Another explained that visiting theatre companies would enable young people to experience and enjoy drama thus facilitating future attendance.

Maybe put them more into school where they see them and then they have got the opportunity to think 'well yes, that was good' and would think about going to it then (female, 18).

4.7.4 Make it social
The sample sometimes noted they might be enticed to cultural events by socially and youth orientated additions, like coffee bars in art galleries and leisure facilities at historic houses.

Heritage *You could probably put like a coffee bar for teenagers to hang out in and they would probably walk in and things and just have a look around and if it was really good then other people would go in and things* (female, 14).

Art *Maybe not make them so quiet, maybe music or something. Yes, music and just make it a bit more lively, a bit more of a social occasion* (female, 14).

4.7.5 Short, sharp and snappy
Dance, drama and music performances typically require the audience to remain in a sedentary position for some time. For an engaged adult this may not be too demanding, but it was noted that an active or restless teenager might exhibit less tolerance.

The solution to this problem therefore was to offer shorter, sharper, more 'snappy' performances which would demand less stamina and perseverance on the part of the audience member.

I have watched ballet on TV before and you sort of stick at it for half an hour and then you just go, 'no, I have had enough'. I think it would have to be … I much prefer much snappier, shorter stuff (male, 18).

4.7.6 A 'modern' content
In every category, there were calls to make events and venues 'more modern': arts and culture were generally perceived as 'old-fashioned' and did not represent today's 'new way of life'.

Art *Probably work that would appeal to them, like pop art stuff, Andy Warhol and things like that, modern art, not really old-fashioned stuff, stuff that would appeal to them* (male, 16).

Music *Make it more modern, instead of going back down to the past to do it* (female, 15).

Along a similar vein, the interviewees felt the arts could by 'lightened up', so that attendance would be 'fun'. One interviewee recalled with pleasure a classical concert for young people, whereby the performance was based around the story of a train, with the orchestra mimicking the various sounds.

Drama   *More plays put forward that are young and fun and bubbly, instead of very serious* (female, 18).

Drama   *Make it fun, not a lot of young people really want to sit there for three hours and watch a really serious play unless they are learning about it* (male, 16).

Others proposed that arts, had to be made cool. During the interviews there were a couple of references to ballet and opera just being 'too embarrassing' to go to. Hence, instilling the 'cool factor' was suggested as a way to dismantle this particular barrier and once attendance had been won at more 'modern' performances, attendance could be expanded to the more traditional forms.

Dance   *I think you have got to make it cool, because if you see break dancing, you always just watch it and you go 'Oh, I wish I could do that' and I have seen other stuff where you are just glued to it. You can easily grab people and say watch this* (male, 18).

4.7.7 Cutting the cost
Bearing in mind the limited finances of most 14–18 year olds, seven of the interviews suggested making events cheaper or offering free tickets.

I think probably lower the prices, because tickets to get in ... if you just wanted to go with a group of friends it would be really, really hard because if they are like £25 for a ticket, then that's quite a lot of money for a child. I think they could maybe offer something that is cheaper (female, 14).

4.7.8 Young performers
Some interviewees felt attendance could be encouraged by using young people as performers, or in the case of art, displaying the work of young artists. In this way, the audience would be able to identify with the event and perhaps feel that the arts were for them.

I think that they should introduce a little section of young artists. I reckon that would be really good because one thing I remember about being a kid was having things forced on you and then you just sort of get sick of it ... but if there's stuff and you can see that this kid is 10 years old and he has done this, it may be really bad, but I think it would be a good thing. You can't really put it next to a van Gogh or anything, but just a little section on its own. I think it would be good and people could say ' yes, this could be a career option for me, I could really get into this now' (male, 18).

4.7.9 Issues of relevance

As well as staging performances by young people, the suggestion was made to create works and performances for young people, specifically in the categories of dance and drama. In order to increase a sense of 'arts ownership', interviewees recommended covering those issues which were of significance to young people, things they cared about.

Dance   *I don't know if you know about the STOMP group, who do it with all the different recycled things, I think that's a really good aspect of doing that, because its like bringing everything of the environment into it and just appealing to young people, what they are bothered about at the moment, so you are sort of focusing on the things that they are interested in* (male, 18).

4.7.10 Take it to the streets

The young people often noted how discomfort and unfamiliarity with traditional venues prohibited attendance. Two interviewees suggested transferring music performances from their usual locations, either to a venue which was frequented by young people or out onto the streets.

The venue would probably be somewhere that young people know, like where bands play and stuff. Maybe playing with bands or something, because its rare that the teenagers are into anything other than pop and rock (female, 17).

I think if you tried to move it away, because you know it's got a kind of stigma attached to it, that you have got to be really upper-class people to listen to it. If you did like ... you know how they did like Shakespeare on the Estate and things like that, where they just move it all onto this council estate and just did it, you could try something like that, just moving classical music into an environment where it can affect people, like more everyday people (male, 18).

4.7.11 Providing the opportunity

The final recommendation for improving attendance mentioned by the sample was simple but fundamental. Throughout the interviews, the perception of cultural venues, was frequently negative, especially among those who had little or no experience of attendance. Yet those who had attended such events found the experience to be predominately positive. The key therefore, was, in some instances, seen to revolve around 'opportunity'. Some interviewees explained that just by giving kids the chance to attend, they would probably appreciate the arts: 'you have got to go once to understand what it's about' (male, 17).

I think if you got half of the kids into somewhere to listen they would appreciate it a lot more, but they just don't get the opportunity (female, 15).

CULTURAL MENTORS?

Kay Kinder and John Harland

The review of previous research confirms that much of young people's involvement in the arts and culture has concentrated on participatory activities, with audience roles considered more rarely. Equally significant, evidence portrays how the young people who do access cultural venues as consumers are more likely to be of a higher social class, female and over 20 years old, suggesting a very wide range of young people who remain outside – excluded or self-excluded – from these opportunities. Investigations into barriers to attendance consistently point up an array of psychological, cultural/social, financial and geographical factors. Yet it is a perceived discomfort with the ambience and the content of a cultural event that appears to be the most pervasive inhibitor to attendance for young people. This may suggest that ensuring young people are at ease in the venue and engaged with the actual aesthetic experience are the two major considerations for cultural inclusion, and indeed the evidence from the audit in Chapter 3 suggests a wide array of activity to address these two aspects.

However, the previous research evidence – and some recent initiatives to increase access of marginalised groups – also points to another important influence upon cultural engagement: namely, the presence of a 'significant other' who provides on-going encouragement and support for that access. Harland et al.'s (1995) idea that arts and culture are 'contagious ... caught off someone else', citing family members (particularly mothers), teachers, and peers as key influences is backed up again by this study's small sample. Equally, the audit of initiatives has shown the use of peers to encourage attendance is burgeoning as an approach to encourage young people's attendance in many organisations and venues.

The other key finding from the small-scale research study relates to the idea of different discourses apparent in the accounts of high and low attenders' experiences of venues. In this way, the differences suggest parallels with the concept of 'motherese' (Ferguson, 1977), a language and communication system between parent and offspring that naturally adapts, changes and grows to match a child's linguistic stage of development. Does cultural engagement also require special (or specially adapted) opportunities to experience the audience role? Does the young person's cultural experience need to be communicated or articulated in some way? Is personalised guidance and modelling of how to perform as – and enjoy being – a 'cultural receiver/re-interpreter' a key factor underpinning sustained attendance? Does, in fact, arts and cultural appreciation develop from experiencing a kind of cultural motherese? And if the young person has lacked or not registered this opportunity, could a mentor or mediator be seen as the surrogate provider of arts/cultural motherese?

If this notion of mediation and support is a potentially effective strategy for helping young people access cultural venues, then the principles and techniques of mentorship, and, in particular, its usage in the context of young people who are disengaged from educational and training opportunities becomes a distinct possibility. The parallels between youngsters excluded and self-excluding from education and those unable or unwilling to access cultural opportunity may not be initially obvious: nevertheless, the strategies undertaken to support the principle of social inclusion may be a productive line of inquiry for those wishing to develop approaches that enhance young people's cultural access.

At a national level, mentoring is now commonly proffered as an essential element of initiatives aimed at reintegrating disaffected youngsters. For example, the Social Exclusion Unit's report 'Truancy and School Exclusion' suggests that mentoring be a '... key component of the individual plans for reintegration of excluded youngsters' (GB. SEU, 1998:26). The Mentoring Bursary programme, established in 1998, is currently supporting 20 projects of mentoring for young people and this is managed by the National Mentoring Network on behalf of the DfEE.

'Mentoring' of course also has many other different meanings and applications, besides work with disengaged youngsters, including staff development in the industrial and commercial workplace. Deriving from the name of 'Mentor' (a friend given charge of Odysseus's son), the idea of a senior, older or more informed person guiding, advising and being a positive role model for someone younger is now well established. The discipline of mentoring in the workplace, with its long tradition in the American world of work, commonly distinguishes between:

- *apprenticeship models*, where work-related skills are shown/modelled and passed on by the mentor in a craftsman tradition; essentially an assimilation approach;
- *competency models*, where the mentor has a systematic and practical trainer or coach role, which essentially involves observation, feedback on pre-defined competencies; and
- *reflective models*, where the mentor helps the mentee examine practice in a non-judgmental and non-hierarchical way: it is characterisable as a joint exploration and sharing of mutual practice within the tradition of 'the mutual friend'.

How far would the concept of cultural mentors fall within any one of these models? The competency model clearly has applications in sports mentoring, with its high performance-related, measurable competency focus, but may seem far removed from arts and cultural appreciation. The idea of peer mentoring clearly lies within the tradition of the reflective model as does the idea of collaborative mentoring by individuals with different arts audience experiences. However, both the apprenticeship and reflective models perhaps also would appear to necessitate some clarification or codification of essential aptitudes or skills; and, as such, may usefully serve as a reminder that being a successful and committed audience member probably equally requires a skill-base. This raises many questions for a cultural mentor role. What exactly does the skilled and experienced arts/cultural receiver do or know? How did they themselves learn to understand the content and protocols of any chosen cultural event? Equally, if audience membership is conceived as a skill, what are the implications for schools and arts pedagogy? How far could cultural mentoring inform practice and approaches within the arts curriculum? Certainly, if cultural attendance needs careful nurturing and the development of a skill-base, the notion that young people's access is 'solved' by ensuring entitlement to one or two performances a year appears somewhat unrealistic and woefully inadequate. Mentoring again may offer a model for that nurturing and on-going support.

Just as for Odysseus's son, the notion of surrogacy for a parent role is perhaps also implicit in the nomenclature of 'mentor'. Certainly the idea of mentoring for disaffected and excluded youngsters as referenced above has that intent. One of the major research studies of a long-standing youth mentoring programme across the USA ('Big Brothers/Big Sisters of America') suggests:

> *Support and guidance from adults are a critical part of the process that allows youth to grow into responsible adults. Yet today, there is a scarcity of such support. The institutions we have historically relied on to provide youth with adult support and guidance – families, schools and neighbourhoods – have changed in ways that have dramatically reduced their capacity to deliver such support.*
> (Tierney et al., 1995:1)

The study acknowledges that 'observations of and interaction with adults and the adult world' are how adolescents form 'fundamental assumptions about society and their potential role in it' and notes how mentoring as a form of social intervention has been advocated in 'such diverse areas as welfare reform, education, violence prevention, school-to-work transition and national service'.

If the mentoring tradition does offer some valuable strategies and approaches for encouraging youth access to cultural venues, the lessons learnt from evaluation and previous research need also to be borne in mind. Successful mentoring schemes are often said to require:

- screening of both the mentor and mentee
- training and orientation for the mentor
- consideration of the matching process to link the right mentor to right mentee
- frequent meetings between mentor and mentee
- supervision of the 'matches' and support for the mentor

American research (Tierney et al., 1995) showed that success particularly occurred where the partnership had high levels of contact (144 hours of direct contact per year) and the mentor role was underpinned by the principle of being a friend who supports rather than expects the young person to change. It was noteworthy that one of the findings of this research was that generic mentoring, while positively affecting achievement in school and decreasing the likelihood of substance abuse, made no impact on attendance at arts and cultural events. From this evidence, it would seem that a specific role of cultural mentor/mediator would be required if increasing arts involvement is a particular goal. Clearly, its value in both formal and informal education still needs further exploration, some bold and imaginative piloting and careful evaluation. However, the evidence throughout this study suggests considerable potential for the concept.

AREAS FOR FURTHER ENQUIRY

6

Concluding statement from the Gulbenkian Foundation and the Arts Council of England

The report indicates that a number of effects result from visits by young people to cultural venues: a more positive attitude towards the arts and culture; reinforced appreciation of the arts; motivation to attend future events; acquisition of knowledge through attendance; psychological well-being; and inspiration to participate in the arts. Young people of all backgrounds, we would hope, would have opportunity to access these benefits.

However, the report also highlights that, despite young people being willing to assume an audience role, only a minority actually reported increased attendance. The report notes that there are various motives for attendance at cultural venues: the acquisition of knowledge, socialising, achieving a sense of psychological well-being, and the aesthetic qualities of the work. At the same time, practical obstacles to attendance, such as cost, travel and lack of time, as well as psychological barriers, are sited.

The relationship between motivation and barriers is a complex issue. Added to this is the fact that the arts sector is wide. It encompasses dance, drama, visual arts and crafts, music, literature, combined arts and new media and involves a medley of partners from cultural venues to schools and communities, the youth service, government bodies, the private sector, and the arts funding system. Furthermore, cultural venues themselves vary: large to small, touring to building-based. Regional differences present further contrasts. Each sector must consider the context in which work with young people is taking place in the light of its own very particular characteristics.

We believe that to offer a series of specific recommendations would be restrictive rather than expansive. Therefore, based upon suggestions elicited from readers of a draft of this report, we have chosen to pose a series of general and broad statements and questions. It is our hope that the various sectors will consider each of these, and develop their own answers and that this process will encourage the debate around how cultural venues can draw in, develop, and maintain the interest of young people.

Young people's involvement

Young people are not a passive component in the equation. They are capable of contributing to the cultural life of venues, the wider community and the country. How can the ideas, aspirations, experiences and opinions of young people themselves be central to and inform all areas of enquiry, those posed below and those that will inevitably arise out of further debate? How can venues interact with the culture of young people?

Profile and commitment

It is critical that the importance of attracting young people to quality arts experiences at cultural venues be recognized both by the venues themselves as well as by schools. How can venues develop this vital link with young people while, at the same time, retaining their commitment to their more traditional audiences? If schools or teachers are reluctant to engage with the arts sector, what can be done to ameliorate this?

Atmosphere and information

Visitors of all ages to cultural venues appreciate a comfortable and welcoming atmosphere and access to clear information. What measures (e.g. building-related concerns, signage, staffing, catering arrangements, marketing, programming, opening hours and ticketing/booking procedures) can be taken by cultural venues to make themselves more inviting to young people on their own as well as with their families?

Bridging

Schools in particular can create bridges between young people and cultural venues. People who regularly attend cultural venues can, as individuals, serve a similar purpose. How can this 'bridging function' be further encouraged, developed and supported? How can better links with families, and particularly those who rarely attend, be fostered?

Context and relevance

The work of cultural venues is more easily accessed when an aspect of it is familiar and relevant to the individual or group. How can the arts in cultural venues be made more familiar and more relevant to young people? How can young people contribute to the process of programming? What can be done to make the work more relevant to non-western cultures? What role does new technology play in attracting, maintaining and developing young people as audience? Is there a particular role for multi-media?

Special schemes and initiatives

There are existing schemes and discrete initiatives developed by various sectors, frequently aimed at increasing motivation for young people to attend venues and/or addressing barriers to attendance. What is the value and role of special schemes and initiatives? How do they best fit into the main work of cultural venues, the work of schools and the youth service and regional and government priorities? How can the momentum of schemes and initiatives be sustained?

Training

Existing, emerging and future areas of work all require training. What specific training is needed – for whom and by whom? What skills, particularly in relation to mentoring, are needed within the arts sector?

Monitoring and evaluation

In order to move any work forward systematically, it is critical to monitor and evaluate. How can 'success' be determined in relation to attracting and maintaining an audience of young people? How can the work be effectively monitored and evaluated?

Sharing

Much good work between cultural venues and young people, supported by other sectors such as schools, the youth service, the arts funding system and government, is taking place. By what means can the effective work already taking place, as well as new and innovative developments of the future, be shared and built upon?

Research

Further research is needed. What possibilities exist for longitudinal studies of specific types of intervention, both within and beyond the school environment, and of their effectiveness? How may the continuum of participation and audience attendance be investigated further?

References

AMCo (NORTHERN ARTS MARKETING) (1993). *An Analysis of Perceived and Actual Barriers to Theatre-Going as Experienced by C1 and C2 Potential Attenders*. Northern Arts.

ANDERSON, D. (1997). *A Common Wealth: Museums and Learning in the United Kingdom. A Report to the Department of National Heritage*. London: Department of National Heritage. 2nd edition (1999) published as *A Common Wealth: Museums in the Learning Age. A Report to the Department for Culture, Media and Sport*. London: HMSO.

ARTS COUNCIL OF ENGLAND (1994). *Youth Audience Research Report*. London: ACE.

ARTS COUNCIL OF ENGLAND (1997). *Leading through Learning: The English Arts Funding System's Policy for Education and Training*. London: ACE.

ARTS COUNCIL OF ENGLAND (1998). *Bringing new art to new people. Arts Council of England announces 'New Audiences' projects*. 21 September, Press release. London: ACE.

ARTS COUNCIL OF ENGLAND (1999). *Arias for all! Opera companies reach out to new people as part of the Arts Council's New Audiences' programme*. 10 February, Press release. London: ACE.

ARTS COUNCIL OF GREAT BRITAIN (1992). *Drama in Schools*. London: ACGB.

ARTS COUNCIL OF GREAT BRITAIN (1993). *Dance in Schools*. London: ACGB.

BEER, V. (1987). 'Great Expectations: do museums know what visitors are doing?', *Curator*, 30, 3: 206–214.

BLUD, L.M. (1990a). 'Social interaction and learning among family groups visiting a museum', *International Journal of Museum Management and Curatorship*, 9: 43–51.

BLUD, L.M. (1990b). 'Sons and Daughters: Observations on the way families interact during a museum visit', *International Journal of Museum Management and Curatorship*, 9: 257–264.

BULL, J. (1993). 'Getting the Message from a School Visit to an Exhibition', *Teaching History*. January: 20ff.

BUTLER, B.H. and SUSSMAN, M.B. (eds.) (1989). *Museums Visits and Activities for Family Life Enrichment*. New York: Haworth Press.

CALOUSTE GULBENKIAN FOUNDATION (1982,1989). *The Arts in Schools: Principles, Practice and Provision*. London: CGF.

CAMPAIGN FOR MUSIC IN THE CURRICULUM (1998). *The Fourth "R": The case for music in the school curriculum*. West Horsley: Music Education Council.

COMMUNITY DEVELOPMENT FOUNDATION (1992). *Arts and Communities: The Report of the National Inquiry into Arts and the Community*. London: CDF Publications.

COOPER, P. and TOWER, R. (1992). 'Inside the consumer mind: consumer attitudes to the arts'. *Journal of the Market Research Society*, 34, 4: 299–311.

DAVIES, S. (1994). *By Popular Demand: A strategic analysis of the market potential for museums and galleries in the UK*. London: Museums and Galleries Commission.

DOWNING, D. (1999). Creative symbiosis: a study of the creative contribution made by audiences to the process of theatre production. Unpublished MA thesis, University of Leeds.

FERGUSON, C.A. (1977). 'Baby talk as a simplified register'. In Snow, C.E. and Ferguson, C.A. (eds.) *Talking to Children*. Cambridge: Cambridge University Press.

FOWLE, K. (1997). *SCRATCH! Free your mind and your art will follow. A project conducted by young people for young people to raise awareness of museums and art galleries in Sussex. Report for work conducted in the project September 1976–June 1997* (mimeo).

GARDNER, H. (1973). *The Arts and Human Development*. New York: John Wiley.

GREAT BRITAIN. DEPARTMENT FOR EDUCATION AND EMPLOYMENT (1998). *Study Support Projects Unlock New Learning Opportunities – Clarke*. 19 October. London: DfEE.

GREAT BRITAIN. DEPARTMENT FOR EDUCATION AND EMPLOYMENT. DEPARTMENT FOR CULTURE, MEDIA AND SPORT. NATIONAL ADVISORY COMMITTEE ON CREATIVE AND CULTURAL EDUCATION. (1999). *All Our Futures: Creativity, Culture and Education*. London: DfEE.

GREAT BRITAIN. DEPARTMENT FOR CULTURE, MEDIA AND SPORT (1999a). *Museums for the Many*. London: DCMS.

GREAT BRITAIN. DEPARTMENT FOR CULTURE, MEDIA AND SPORT (1999b). *Policy Action Team 10: A Report to the Social Exclusions Unit – Arts and Sports*. London: DCMS.

GREAT BRITAIN. DEPARTMENT OF NATIONAL HERITAGE (1996). *Setting the Scene: The Arts and Young People*. London: DNH.

GREAT BRITAIN. HMI (1991). *A survey of the use of museums by 16–19 year olds*. London: DES.

GREAT BRITAIN. OFFICE FOR NATIONAL STATISTICS (1999). *Social Trends 29*. London: HMSO.

GREAT BRITAIN. SOCIAL EXCLUSIONS UNIT (1998). *Truancy and School Exclusion Report by the Social Exclusion Unit*. London: HMSO.

HARGREAVES, D.H. (1983). 'Dr. Brunel and Mr. Dunning: reflections on aesthetic knowing'. In ROSS, M. (ed.): *The Arts: a Way of Knowing*. Oxford: Pergamon Press.

HARLAND, J. and KINDER, K. (1995). 'Buzzes and barriers: young people's attitudes to participation in the arts', *Children and Society*, 9, 4: 15–31.

HARLAND, J., KINDER, K. and HARTLEY, K. (1995). *Arts in Their View: A Study of Youth Participation in the Arts*. Slough: NFER.

HARLAND, J., KINDER, K, HAYNES, J. and SCHAGEN, I. (1998). *The Effects and Effectiveness of Arts Education in Schools: Interim Report 1*. Slough: NFER.

HARLAND, J., KINDER, K., HARTLEY, K. and WILKIN, A. (1996). *Attitudes to Participation in the Arts, Heritage, Broadcasting and Sport: A Review of Recent Research*. London: DNH.

HARRIS QUALITATIVE (1997). *Children as an Audience for Museums and Galleries*. Prepared for the Arts Council and the Museums and Galleries Commission.

HARRIS RESEARCH CENTRE (1993a). *Black and Asian Attitudes to the Arts in Birmingham*. London: ACGB.

HARRIS RESEARCH CENTRE (1993b). *Orchestral Concerts: Qualitative Research*. London: ACGB.

HILL, R. (1997). *The Arts, Commercial Culture and Young People: Factors Affecting Young People's Participation in Artistic and Cultural Programmes*. Council of Europe Directorate of Education, Culture and Sport.

HOGARTH, S., KINDER, K., and HARLAND, J. (1997). *Arts Organisations and their Education Programmes*. London: ACE.

HOOD, M.G. (1989). 'Leisure Criteria of Family Participation and Non-participation in Museums'. In BUTLER AND SUSSMAN (1989), op. cit.:151ff.

HORNBROOK, D. (1991). *Education in Drama*. London: Falmer.

INGS, R. with JONES, R. and RANDALL, N. (1998). *Mapping Hidden Talent: investigating youth music projects*. Leicester: National Youth Agency.

McMANUS, P. (1987). 'It's the company you keep... the social determination of learning-centred behaviour in a science museum', *International Journal of Museum Management and Curatorship*, 6: 263–70.

MARWICK, S. (1994). 'Out of the mouths of babes', *Museums Journal*, October.

MASS OBSERVATION LTD (1990). *Arts in London: A Survey of Users and Non-Users*. GLA.

MATHERS, K. (1996). *Museums, galleries amid new audiences*. London: *Art and Society*.

MAX (1998). *Youth Research: Presentation of Findings*. Oxford: Marketing the Arts in Oxfordshire.

MOORE, J. (1997). *Poverty: Access and Participation in the Arts*. Dublin: Combat Poverty Agency/Arts Council.

NATIONAL CAMPAIGN FOR THE ARTS (1998). 'Evidence to the National Advisory Committee on Creative and Cultural Education' [online]. Available at: http://www.artscampaign.org/robinson.htm [26 April, 1999].

NATIONAL CAMPAIGN FOR THE ARTS (1999). 'Encouraging Access' [online]. Available at: http://www.artscampaign.org/access.htm [26 April, 1999].

O'BRIEN, J. (1996). *Secondary School Pupils and the Arts: Report of a MORI research study*. London: ACE.

O'NEILL, C. (1989). 'Ways of Seeing: Audience function in drama and theatre', *2D*, 8, 2: 16–29.

OFFICE FOR STANDARDS IN EDUCATION (1998). *The Arts Inspected*. Oxford: Heinemann.

PRENTICE, R. (1994). 'Perceptual deterrents to visiting museums and other heritage attractions', *International Journal of Museum Management and Curatorship*, 13: 264–279.

RESEARCH SERVICES OF GREAT BRITAIN (1991). *RSGB Omnibus Survey. Report on a survey of arts and cultural activities in GB*. London: ACE.

RESEARCH SURVEYS OF GREAT BRITAIN (1994). *Orchestral Concerts: Quantitative Research*. London: ACE.

RICHEY, S. (1996). 'Two-way culture.' Paper presented at the Council of Europe Colloquium, Varazden, Croatia. October.

RIDER, S. (1997). *Off the Wall*. Commissioned from Artswork by the Arts Council of England (mimeo).

RIDER, S. and ILLINGWORTH, S. (1997). *Museums and Young People*. Commissioned from Artswork by the Museums Association, London.

ROGERS, R. (1995a). *Guaranteeing an Entitlement to the Arts in Schools*. London: RSA.

ROGERS, R. (1995b). 'In need of a guarantee.', *Children and Society*, 9, 4: 32–51.

ROSS, M. and KAMBA, M. (1997). *The State of The Arts in Five English Secondary Schools*. Exeter: University of Exeter.

ROYAL SOCIETY FOR THE ENCOURAGEMENT OF ARTS, MANUFACTURES AND COMMERCE (1997). *The Arts Matter*. Aldershot: Gower.

SECONDARY HEADS ASSOCIATION (1998). *Drama Sets You Free*. London: SHA.

SELWOOD, S., CLIVE, S. and IRVING, D. (1995). *An Enquiry into Young People and Art Galleries*. London: *Art and Society*.

SELWOOD, S. with TRAYNOR, J. (1998). *Tate Gallery Visitor Audit 11*. London: Tate Gallery (unpublished report).

SHARP, C. and DUST. K. (1997). *Artists in Schools: A Handbook for Teachers and Artists*. Slough: NFER.

SYSTEM THREE (1998). *Attendance at, Participation in, and Attitudes Towards the Arts in Scotland: Final Report*. Edinburgh: SAC.

TIERNEY, J.P., GROSSMAN, J.B. with RESCH, N.L. (1995). *Making a Difference: An Impact Study of Big Brothers/Big Sisters*. Philadelphia: Public/Private Ventures.

TILLEY, B. (1997). *Between The Eyes*. Oldham: Oldham Art Gallery (mimeo).

VERGE, B. (1994). 'Through the eyes of a child', *Museums Journal*, October.

WHITFIELD, W. (1991). *Working with the arts: Case studies of six youth arts projects*. Leicester: Youth Work Press.

WILLIS, P. (1990). *Moving Culture: An enquiry into the cultural activities of young people*. London: CGF.

WILSON, B. (1997). *The Quiet Evolution: Changing the Face of Arts Education*. Los Angeles: The Getty Education Institute for the Arts.

WOLINS, I.S. (1989). 'A Case for Family Programs in Museums'. In BUTLER AND SUSSMAN (1989), op. cit.

WOOD, R. (1990). 'Museum learning: a family focus'. In DURBIN, G. (ed.) for the Group for Education in Museums (1996). *Developing Museums Exhibitions For Lifelong Learning*. London: HMSO: 77ff.

XANTHOUDAKI, M. (1998). 'Is it always worth the trip? The contribution of museum and gallery educational programmes to classroom art education', *Cambridge Journal of Education*, 28, 2: 181–95.

YERK, R. (1984). 'Families. What are we doing for our largest audience?' *American Association of Zoological Parks and Aquariums Annual Conference Proceedings*: 380–386.